Imoh "Son of David"

The Ultimate Curse On Mankind

Editions Dedicaces

THE ULTIMATE CURSE ON MANKIND

Copyright © 2015 by Editions Dedicaces LLC

All rights reserved. No part of this book may be used or reproduced in any form whatsoever without written permission except in the case of brief quotations embodied in critical articles or reviews.

Published by:
    Editions Dedicaces LLC
    12759 NE Whitaker Way, Suite D833
    Portland, Oregon, 97230
    www.dedicaces.us

Library of Congress Cataloging-in-Publication Data
  "Son of David", Imoh
    The Ultimate Curse On Mankind / by Imoh "Son of David".
    p. cm.
    ISBN-13: 978-1-77076-548-1 (alk. paper)
    ISBN-10: 1-77076-548-4 (alk. paper)

Imoh "Son of David"

The Ultimate Curse On Mankind

Appreciation

Numerous people I would have loved to thank because of their support and influence on the book, but the space won't be enough for all. I would love to thank my publisher Guy Boulianne for accepting to publish my work, my community of friends and love ones. I am grateful for your support.

Introduction

Man And His Quest For The Unknown And Supernatural

From prehistoric times through the stone and medieval ages to the advent of civilization, man has over the centuries shown his inseparable penchant to believe in the supernatural and unseen forces or beings. It is fair to assume that it is an integral primitive part of the human psyche to believe in the supernatural and the invisible. From Gods to Devils, Angels to demons, super-strength humans, mermaids and Atlantis beings, spirits, fairies, ghosts, vampires, werewolves, etc. the list is endless. Different cultures, ethnicities, have evolved, and each having its own doctrine, dogma, myth, tradition and believe of one form of supernatural force or figure, thus the birth of religion.

Whether true or false if any of the religious doctrines hold water, one thing is certain; religion has divided mankind against itself. It has robbed man of his true sense of reasoning, magnified his stupidity, hostility and bitterness towards his fellow men in both subtle and avowed ways.

Religion gives man a pious hope/wish for the unseen and unrealistic future of life after death which cannot be proven beyond any reasonable doubt of its existence. Unlike a simple law of science like the Newton's law of gravity; "whatever goes up must come down", which is very practical anywhere on earth, religious beliefs have no prove. In other words, religion is a doctrine of baseless dogmas and the mother of all clueless fanaticism. Religion has done more harm than racism, anti-Semitism and apartheid put together. As a matter of fact you can't ignore a touch of religion in the mentioned.

Religion which claims to try to better the society and impose what is just, has done the very opposite. History has shown us that wars and lives have been fought and lost in the name of religion. Religion makes a person dislike another simply because he or she doesn't think or share the same dogmas with him. For religion will label the different individual: "SINNER, INFIDEL, ENEMY OF GOD, etc" as the case may be. It is no longer news that countries which are most viewed to be very religious are often the least developed, corrupt, with high rate of insurgency, crime and insecurity, poverty, human rights abuse, women and children abuse e.g. Nigeria, Liberia, Ghana, Iraq, Pakistan, Somalia, Afghanistan, North and South Sudan, etc. while the most developed nations are not as religious as any of the mentioned countries, their advancement and progress is nothing compared to the former. This is absolutely not a coincidence. If religion was beneficiary and morally and economically rewarding then we should have seen its fruit in the above mentioned religious countries. Why on earth will countries like Sweden with an agnostic population of about 85%, Denmark 80%, Japan 65%, Norway 72%, France 54%, and South Korea 52% be more developed and prosperous than any of these nations? The answer is simple; Religion is anti-progress and anti-sense. It discourages reason and the use of the acumen and intuition by its adherents and followers. It has never brought any real development and betterment to mankind.

Religion through its institutions has over the centuries murdered, threatened and antagonize scientists, thinkers and researchers of old whose discoveries were not in tandem with their medieval hokum.

If mankind never had education and science but only religion, we would have still been in the Stone Age practicing barbarism and superstition. But if mankind had just science and education but no religion, the world would have known more peace, development and civilization than what it is today.

It is generally observed that man is a greedy, insecure, manipulative and atrocious creature. Even without religion, we'll still have evil people doing evil things. People will still commit murder and plunder their kind. But a man has never been so enthusiastic in buffoonery, justified in callousness and so happy in stupidity like when he is acting under religious principles, laws and guidance. Religion gives man the ultimate cover and excuse to plunder other men at ease. Religion is the ultimate inspiration for men to use and witch-hunt their kind, manipulate them and enslave them. Religion easily makes good people participate in evil and make bad men more dangerous. With religion, the innocent man becomes more sheepish and the Machiavellian will be more than willing to accept this opportunism with open arms. Religion will never make a man good. If it did, the time when religion ruled the world would not be called "THE DARK AGE", and the most religious nations would have been the most peaceful and crime-free nations, but we are still wishing on it.

The concept of humanism and an all encompassing neighborliness and peaceful world is nothing but a chimera so far religion lives among us. Religion is a social cancer on mankind. Any concept or ideology that promotes a "WE versus THEM", or creates separation and classification of people into protagonists and antagonists, heroes versus villains, the good guys versus the bad guys, such ideology is a turpitude and must not be embraced at all. Religion is the mother of all ideologies that classifies humans into the echelon of friends and foes.

To the Muslim, the Christians, Buddhists, Jews, agnostics, atheists, irreligious, etc are infidels, sinners, enemies of Allah, ignorant, najis (filthiest thing possible), condemned, etc. And to the Christian: the Muslim, Buddhists, Jews, agnostics, atheists, irreligious and all others are satanic, blind, foolish, ignorant, condemned, etc.

On the other hand, the atheists, agnostics, irreligious, secularists and humanists are telling them that such an ideology is flawed, unnecessary and dangerous to us all, but the religious insists that anyone who wishes to promote unity, the rejection of their divisive ideologies is an enemy willy-nilly. How can humanity ever know peace, progress and good neighborliness as long as religion still lives?

The Truth-meter

What makes something true?
A. Because a billion people believe it?
B. People are willing to die for it?
C. It feels absolutely right?
D. People you respect say its true?
E. It is supported by valid evidence?

"Religion is about turning untested beliefs into unshakeable truth through the power of institutions and the passage of time." – Richard Dawkins

---

FROM SUPERSTITION TO RELIGION

I don't know why people of this digital age will allow manuscripts written by people who wrote on stones 6,000 years ago and more to tell them about an invisible being in the sky. The same people who said the earth is flat, worked with bulls on farmlands, drew water from the well, hunt with spears and arrows, etc are the ones we derive our views on God in the 21st century? The concept of God which is highly revered by most people is merely conceptualized ideologies from ancient manuscripts authored by people whose knowledge of science of the earth and other things has been proven wrong.

God was thought up by men who were no more intelligent than us, and that's why their holy story does not stand up to scrutiny. These people rode on horses; as such they will tell you God rides on a horse or will ride on a horse on the last day. Today we ride horses for sports, but drive Buggattis and Benzes and fly with Boeings. I don't know if the God in holy books still ride on horses and hasn't upgraded? They reared goats, sheep and cattle for livelihood; they'll tell you God will bless you with farm animals. Today we drill oil, do stock exchange, online trading, etc. Will that same "God" have the mindset of blessing you with goats and cattle? Their enemies were lions and other wild carnivores; they'll tell you the devil is a "beast" with long claws and ugly looking eyes and tail. But we all know the "Devil" of these present times is well dressed in Prada and Gucci suits.

They practiced polygamy; as such they tell you God will give you plenty of wives and virgins in heaven. But we all know civilization has come of age and no woman wants to be treated as second place. Women had no place of respect in the society of their time, so they tell you how God uses only the men (prophets and disciples) and that a woman is the devil's favorite tool and a lower being to man. They came up with several acclaimed divine laws making their God a misogynistic being and the anti-women clauses in their holy books were grafted to permanently reduce the place of the woman and make the man superior. Since the authors of these scripts came from the Middle East (Jews and Arabs), then it is not surprising that all the prophets of God they'll tell you about came from their geographical clime, including the son of God. Taking further their jingoism and ego boost, they assert that every other belief or perspective about God aside theirs is from the DEVIL; this is jingoism at its perfection!

"All men are born with a nose and ten fingers, but no none was born with a knowledge of God"- Voltaire

The religion one might have been born into was no divine plan, but a mere geographical accident of birth. If you were born in Saudi Arabia there is 98% chance you'll be a Muslim. If you were born in Japan, there is an 80% chance you'll be irreligious, and if you were born in Southern Nigeria, there is a 95% chance you'll be a Christian. And there you are, thinking to yourself that the religion you are born into just happens to be the true and correct religion because you are some kind of special individual in some kind of divine plan, right?

Many religious folks especially the monotheistic adherents frown at the irreligious and atheism is unaware of the fact that their atheism status is roughly 95- 99%. They rejected over 8,000 Gods and different religions just to uphold theirs as true and infallible. This is merely a grandeur in imaginary beings and weightless creeds. The other religious adherents share the same disaffection on your God and religion. Your belief in one creed and God doesn't by any chance erase your condemnation in other doctrines just as your belief is certain that none but yours is sacrosanct.

Your belief in another God doesn't afford you some importance in the eyes of thousand other religions on earth or their God(s). And you are not anywhere important and respected by their God(s). You are simply a step away from atheism; you are one god ahead of the atheist. It is just remaining one more god to reject and become like those you always condemn. Besides, you are already condemning those worshipping a different God.

The theist and the religious man assert that the universe was created by God and God alone. It's amazing how the word of God has to be written down by men. God needed not men before he created the universe and billions of galaxies and stars therein, so they say. But somehow God suddenly needs men to write down his words and cut down millions of trees to print his holy books. Does it not make sense that if God needed not men in creating nature, as they claim, he surely need no men in writing his words and speaking on his behalf? Sometimes I wonder if these religious people are describing the God they believe in or they are just describing themselves. God is nothing but the alter-ego of superstitious men.

What men call God is not different from a dead person. Friedrich Nietzche said 'God is dead", this explains the need to hide him in the cloak of invisibility and so called spirituality. The dead cannot talk, write nor do anything for themselves, the same characteristics is exhibited by your God, it's always men doing the writing and talking for him. As a matter of fact, when one dies, he becomes closer to God because they both won't exist.

I am of the opinion that no one can prove the existence God just like no one can prove the existence an invisible bathroom inside Mount Everest. Thus, it is necessary to disprove anything ascribed to God(s). As for me, God does not exist, because if he did, he would have made himself well known and clear-up all doubts, controversies and fallacies about his name. But he hasn't done that and he is never going to do that, and because of this, it is only reasonable to debunk a being who has never made himself available, known, and provable to all. Anyone can cook up any deity that satisfies his fancy but none has been able to prove its existence.

Having critically examined the Abrahamic information booklets and instructional manuals otherwise known as the holy books, the claims regarding the nature, attributes, characteristics and methodology of God, has led to my conclusion that the existence of such a deity posit a logical improbability and that His/her/Its nature and characteristics present a contradiction in all terms and principles . One cannot assert convincingly with any mathematical exactitude and realistic probability that such a God exists. However, if in the unlikely event that a God as epitomized and expressed in the Abrahamic texts exists, I renounce being a member of His/Her/Its fan club. Perhaps He/She/It has been grossly misrepresented and seditiously described, but such a deity is not deserving of any reasonable man's adoration.

Perfection is a flaw in existence. Imperfection is inherent to existence. For something to exist it is imperfect; it must have flaws. Flawlessness is only found in the non-existence. I am told that flawlessness is among the many characteristics of God. Hence, if God exists, then he is imperfect and flawed. If he is perfect, that automatically translates that he is a non-existing entity. His existence is only conceivable in the human mind and his perfection is only asserted in the so called holy books authored by men, which still translates to a fiction of the mind (the only place where perfection is tangible). I personally think it will be daft for me to accept what a man has thought-up within himself or claimed to have received as a "word of God" without any evidence.

People live as if religion is necessary for life. But that is because they have never tried living without it. Man was not born with religion, only with the tendency to oppress and subject his fellow man through subversion and mental manipulation. A life without religion is possible, even if not chosen. The ultimate path of knowledge man should follow and embrace is science. Because science has credibility on its predictions, theories, formulations, laws and in solving human problems. It is safe to follow scientific explanations of the Universe than some story of a talking snake and naked woman in a garden. Ricky Gervais had this to say, which I equally share in the sentiment:

"Science seeks truth. And it does not discriminate. For better or worse it finds things out. Science is humble. It knows what it knows and it knows what it doesn't know. It bases its conclusions and beliefs on hard evidence.... Evidence that is constantly updated and upgraded. It doesn't get offended when facts come along. It embraces the body of knowledge. It does not hold medieval practices because they are traditional."

Before your religion came there were others and now they are no longer in vogue. Different religions come and go but the universe and humanity will always be here. Until we know the definitive truth about the very beginning; and until we answer the original questions without a doubt, religion will remain fraudulent. Religion will continue to promise us that we will find the answers only when we die. Science is the only one trying to find answers to these questions while we are still alive. And science is the only one trying to get to the very beginning and empirically show it to us for the very first time. It may take science one million years to get there. But I am rooting for science not religion.

Science is a superior way of thinking and providing solution and answers to problems. Accepting that there will always be questions and problems is wiser than thinking you have all the answers. Science may not answer everything satisfactorily, but everything has a scientific explanation. And that is much better than claiming to have absolute answers and getting them embarrassingly wrong.

The question should not be "can science answer everything?" The question ought to be "has religion answered anything correctly?" The answer to the question is a plain "no". Religion provides no greater knowledge and convincing information of any value.

The objections that science can't answer everything is like complaining that a car isn't fast enough, and then turn around offering riding on the back of a tortoise as an alternative means of transportation. Religion is a cripple way of thinking and a bizarre way of solving any problem.

Religion can and does explain everything and anything. But it's always embarrassing wrong. There will always be questions and science is the most effective way to keep finding the best answers and keep updating the outdated ones. If it gets is wrong, it is not is not afraid in correcting its previous summation. But religion is sacrosanct, whether or not it discovered it was wrong. Man was meant to ask questions, think, discover, invent and find practical solutions to problems; this is only possible with science. With religion, thinking and questioning is nil.

"Prejudices are what fools use for reason"-
Voltaire

Is It A Fool That Does Not Believe In A God?

"Only a fool says there is no God", is a phrase religious adherents are in a habit of regurgitating. Such despotism in verbiage is what made Voltaire say "Prejudice is what fools use in reasoning". To make such an arrogant assertion would desire an unshakeable prove. To say that only fools disbelief in a God is to imply that the wise believe in a God. More than 70% of the world's population believe in the existence of God, which in other words means that the 70% of the human population are wise beings (I wish it was true), which is only plausible in the grave, unless of course you are referring to another world.

To put it mildly, the most stupid and unreasonable things I've heard people say are always in partnership with God. For example Iranian Cleric Hojatoleslam Kazem Seddiqi said **"Many women, who do not dress modestly... lead young men astray, corrupt their chastity and spread adultery in society, which increases earthquakes."** The Catholic Church's decision against Galileo Galilei read: **"The doctrine that the earth is neither the centre of the universe nor immovable, but moves even with a daily rotation, is absurd, and both philosophically and theologically false, and at least an error of faith"**. And these are the supposedly wise people?

The recent Ebola virus outbreak in West Africa revealed the depth of the wisdom of the patronizers of God. Men of God in Liberia wasted no time in announcing that the Ebola virus outbreak is as a result of the activities of gays and lesbians in the country which has angered God to punish them for their sins. The Liberian Council of Churches said in a statement that the Ebola outbreak has Biblical implications. "God is angry with Liberia," the religious leaders said, according to the Daily Observer.

"Ebola is a plague. Liberians have to pray and seek God's forgiveness over the corruption and immoral acts (such as homosexualism, etc.) that continue to penetrate our society. The African theists were not alone in this enviable theistic show of wisdom in theocratic diagnosis and prognosis. An American Christian radio host who robustly looks for parallels of theocratic roots that the world will come to an end equally joined his West African counterparts to assert that the Ebola epidemic is on a mission from the divine to cleanse the American society of homosexuals. "It may be the great attitude adjustment that I believe is coming," said the American broadcaster, Rick Wiles. "Ebola could solve America's problems with atheism, homosexuality, sexual promiscuity, pornography, and abortion." he continued. "Better make sure the blood of Jesus is upon you, you better make sure you have been marked by the angels so that you are protected by God," Wiles warned. "If not, you may be a candidate to meet the Grim Reaper." When something tragic happens, the religious waste no time in shouting end-time and reconciling the occurrence of such with their primitive texts. I do not understand why they still hold obstinately to the end-time paranoia and choose to buy new gadgets and technological inventions when released into the market. If the end is near, why not bequeath all your money and properties to me or any other total stranger? Clowns! End-time simply means the time when people are being tormented by their ignorance and that time is everyday in places where people have abandoned their sense of reasoning.

When the first recorded case of the Ebola virus was announced in Nigeria, there was hysteria in the air. All manner of rumors impregnated by ignorance, sorry, theocratic wisdom began inseminating in numbers. Nothing is more dangerous like when ignorance is given the blessings of a superstitious fold. We are in an age of social media technology; ignorance found a comfortable passenger seat in the Nigerian social media clime. The famous of all was when information went viral that salt will immune one from contacting the Ebola virus. The prognoses of this unknown source of costly ignorance advised people to bath with salt in their water and drink salt-solution. The government through the ministry of health and information sent out news to counter the rumor but it was late; 2 persons were reported to have died from high blood pressure and 20 more hospitalized over excessive consumption of salt and bitter kola to immune themselves from the Ebola virus.

While the rational people were still battling with the shameful reality of the level of gullibility and mass national ignorance in their clime, a young lady, Paula Asindi, lashed out to defend the salt bath hogwash: "**.... To those who have taken it upon themselves to be Ebola critics, calling those of us who followed the salt-solution exercise all sorts of names: people seem to forget that it isn't a medical prescription, rather it is a spiritual exercise revealed by God to his Prophet (name withheld). We seem to forget that the ways of the Lord are not our ways. He did give a blind man sight in the bible by using mud and saliva; very unorthodox, right? If you ever choose to ignore this spiritual exercise because you feel you have degrees than Jesus or you are just too educated and technologically advanced to be salty, cool. Keep your reservations to yourself and don't make others feel bad. I tell you most solemnly that if Noah had built an ark in our time, he surely would have sailed alone. It is our prayer that as it is in the word of God, the sickness of the Egyptians shall not visit the children of God. Amen!"**

When a society has these kinds of people in intimidating numbers, an Ebola virus epidemic is the least of the problems they should worry about when ignorance is already dealing with them with no remorse. Fear reveals the cost of ignorance. When fear meets ignorance, the consequence from such an encounter is usually sordid. The consequences of stupidity cannot be over-estimated.

Tamale, a place in Ghana, had not seen rain for a while. In the characteristic wisdom of the religious, the theists in that clime diagnosed that it has refused to rain in Tamale because of so much sexual sins. Moral inquisitors specifically cited that the leaked nude pictures and videos of about 50 women who were filmed performing with a Tamale-born Ghanaian based in Canada, is responsible for the unfavorable weather in the metropolis.

A young Nigerian postgraduate student by name Chibuihem Amalaha came to the media and announced that God has given him the wisdom to scientifically proof that same-sex marriage is wrong using magnets. He simply cited that the bar magnet which has the North and South poles is often seen to repel like poles and attract unlike poles. "If you bring two South Poles together, you will find that the two South Poles will not attract indicating that same sex marriage should not hold." he said. "We have seen that the female of a fowl is called hen and the male of a fowl is called a cock. We have never seen where a cock is having sex with a cock and we have never seen where a hen is having sex with another", he asserted. He further claimed that he is the first person on earth to scientifically show that same-sex marriage is wrong, adding: "In general, same sex marriage is evil." According to him in an interview, his professor in the university found the idea very remarkable and told him he could win a Nobel Prize for this. If it is true as this man claimed, then it is obvious he took the professor's sarcasm for a compliment, because I find it difficult to imagine that a science professor can actually believe that this embarrassment can pass for a Nobel Prize unless he is a professor of theology or theological science.

Don't be mistaken to think he is on a world of his own. He has more than enough support that this is in fact wisdom from God. There are many people who are believers of God that will certainly pass his statement for omniscience. Obviously, he is from the part of the world where a large number of believing people are unaware that over 1,000 species of life forms engage in homosexuality ranging from primates to smaller species like worms, this include: domestic cats, dolphins, Chimpanzee, dog, Giraffe, goat, horse, Koala, lion, chicken, raven, rattle snakes, bedbug, cockroach, housefly, etc just to name a handful. I certainly agree with the words of Martin Luther King, Jr. that: **"Nothing in all the world is more dangerous than sincere ignorance and conscientious stupidity"**.

Let's look at the opinion of the religious and theologian in another issue, earthquake:

WHAT CAUSES EARTHQUAKE?

Religious scholars, the men of God, the ones filled with the knowledge of God; men who are well versed with the knowledge of the "greatest" books and beliefs on earth gave the answers below:

"The persecution (of Jews and Torah scholars) caused earthquake"- Shlomo Moshe Amar (Rabbi)

"The slaughter of cows: the main cause of earthquake"- Mohan Bajan (Hindu scholar/priest)

"Many women who do not dress modestly..... lead young men astray, corrupt their chastity and spread adultery in society, which increases earthquakes"- Hojatoleslam Kazem Sedighi (Muslim Cleric)

"The acceptance of homosexuality could result in hurricanes, earthquakes tornadoes, terrorist"- Pat Robertson (Christian preacher)

"It is caused by end time prophecy"- General Christians

"Daddy, what is tectonic plate and seismic activity?" Asked Dhruv, the 9 year old child of Naveen Tummala, an Orthopedic surgeon and a freethinker.

Religious beliefs must be awesome in brilliance and superior in knowledge, very useful it is. You have contributed so much positively to planet earth with your "wisdom of God" and understanding of mysteries. We appreciate your inputs. Please, when next are you going to give us an explanation for the meteorites and comets? Have you heard about the Bermuda triangle? I am sure you have an explanation..... it must be the golf course of Satan or where the 7 headed will emerge from on the last day, right? Please educate us more, we can't do without your profound knowledge on nature. Yours sincerely, the number one fan of theology.

Men do the most stupid things in the name of belief in a God like blowing up themselves and causing terrorism, eating grass to get closer to God, speaking in unintelligible words, accusing their neighbors of all imaginary crimes like witchcraft, demonism, etc, a black person thinking he is an Israeli, legalizing pedophilia, killing homosexuals, etc. I am sure this is what wise people do, right?

The truth is that the fool rhetoric and verse was meticulously grafted to masturbate the ego of the believer into mental grandeur. And to say that anyone who is in a habit of quoting this phrase/verse should consider himself the one charmed by foolery is indeed an undeserved euphemism. The wise man is one who fashions his beliefs in tandem with evidence and reality.

It's rather unfortunate that in the 21st century there exist some people who consider themselves wise because they "Believe" in a God, not because they can prove or ascertain beyond reasonable doubt that there is a God, and those who fashion their belief base on evidence and sound reason are considered "FOOLS".

In this 21st century, the sine qua non of measuring wisdom is in the belief of God, how tragic! How miserable are those who hold sway to this spurious self-delusion rhetoric. For it is obvious the inventors of the rhetoric wanted to help boost the egos of the inept. The late Osama Bin Laden and the bunch of other jihadists all over the world believe in God, hence they are wise. The pedophiles believe in God hence, they are wise. The preachers who milk their congregations believe in God hence they are wise, the priests that rape little children believe in God, hence they are wise. West African Countries like Nigeria and Ghana are die hard believers of God and of course we can see the fruits of their wisdom in their economy and citizenry, which obviously makes them wiser than countries with more than 42% agnostic population such as South Korea, Sweden, France, etc. What an awesome yardstick to determine a wise man. Wisdom Indeed!

Just another thought: Why didn't they say "It is only a FOOL that says there is no SATAN"? Actually the true FOOL is the person who cannot prove the reality of his/her God.

The fact is this: TRUTH does not rely upon prejudiced rhetoric, antagonism and defamatory phrases e.g. "ANTI-CHRIST", "BLASPHEMY", "FOOL", for support. My friend Tavian Oladapo puts it succinctly: Blasphemy is a word made up by those afraid of scrutiny. You cannot claim absolute truth, knowledge and wisdom and then ban scrutiny. It is like claiming you are wearing a bullet proof suit but no one is allowed to shoot at it or test your claims. It is not difficult to imagine why words like blasphemy and heresy were invented. It is odious to make claims and ban reasoning at the same time; it is just an unacceptable primitive quod.

Learn to use your mind to think and reason; it won't get you killed. There is no barrier in the mind except the ones you impose on yourself. Allow yourself fly mentally, you are bigger than what you think. There is no voodoo in thinking! Learn to see things from another view by consciously exercising questions like "why", "how", "when", "where", "what if" in all matters.

Nobody gets taxed from reasoning. The one thing that has no boundary is the mind; don't bind it. Don't create rules for her. Let your creativity spring forth. Allow her to find new ways; release her to entertain herself, for she does not know territories, don't teach it to her. Don't allow anyone, anything and circumstances dictate it to you. There is no such thing as a "no-go-area" in the mind; be free, be human, be creative. If your mind only thinks in a certain kind of way, then you are not thinking. You are merely operating on a script.

You think, therefore you are. You reason therefore you are human. If you think not, therefore you are not. If you do not reason then you are a vegetable.

An article by Daniel Bastes published on the dailymail.co.uk stated:

Atheists have higher IQ's: their intelligence makes them more likely to dismiss religion as irrational and unscientific. According to a US study, atheists tend to be more intelligent than religious people.

Researchers found that those with high IQs had greater self-control and were able to do more for themselves- so did not need the benefits religion provides. They also have better self esteem and built more supportive relationships, the study authors said.

The conclusion was the result of a review of 63 scientific studies about religion and intelligence dating between 1928 and 2012. In 53 of these there was a reliable negative relation between intelligence and religiousity. In just 10 was that relationship positive.

The report went ahead to say that even among children, the more intelligent a child was, the more probable it was that they would shun the church.

The psychologists from the University of Rochester behind the study, defined intelligence **as the ability to reason, plan, solve problems, think abstractly, comprehend complex ideas, learn quickly and learn from experience.**

In their conclusion, they said: "most extant explanations (of a negative relation) share one central theme- the premise that religious beliefs are irrational, not anchored in science, not testable and therefore, unappealing to intelligent people who "know better".

Atheists score higher on IQ tests than religious people according to some research. Does this mean that people accept religious beliefs because they are dimwitted? Not necessarily, says Nigel Barber on an article on huffpost.

"Whether intelligence causes people to reject religious belief is more complex. It is certainly plausible that highly intelligent people would have a problem accepting some of the more improbable beliefs required by their church. Moreover, modern science offers explanations for phenomena that were previously explained exclusively in terms of religion and intelligent people may prefer the scientific account." Nigel's article highlighted.

My view is this: it doesn't take a genius to know that there is no invisible man in the sky. I cannot see any sophistication in calling a spade a spade. I am not certain whether religion reduces the IQ of an individual for we have had several inventors who held allegiance to religious doctrines. But I do wonder whether it is the hallmark of the less intelligent to find religious creed more comforting and attractive. I am certain by observation and social experience that people do and say the most stupid and irrational things because of their religious beliefs and they are more willing to establish an excuse for their irrational and dogmatic sentiments from their religious tenets with strong convictions, thus, making them uncreative, shallow-minded and complacent in their mental enterprise.

The inability of the religious to picture things outside the world of his dogmatic beliefs is the best proof that religion is a checkmate of imagination and a vaccine against novelty. The cognition of a highly religious man does not necessarily go any further than this dictated imagination and explanation from religious creed. And of one the example is a person absolutely holding on the assertion that "A FOOL SAYS THERE IS NO GOD".

A reasonable individual will definitely know that such statement is nothing more than a witless rhetoric of unsophisticated arrogance thrown at the wind, which is no different from saying "Only fool says a pig is not a bird".

"One maybe asked "how can you prove God doesn't exist?" One may reply that it is scarcely necessary to disprove what has never been proved" – David A. Spitz

---

MAGNUM EST VERITAS PRAE VELEBIT. Translation: "THE TRUTH SPEAKS FOR ITSELF". A simple scientific law of gravitation does not rely on emotional rhetoric to prove itself to be true, just throw an object up and it'll come down, simple. Science didn't threaten anyone that does not believe in the law of gravity as "ANTI-GRAVITY", they just left it open to be contested and if you can prove them wrong, then bravo! If you ask me, that is GOD, because it's evidential, credential and unquestionable. But religion hides under the cover of phrases like "BLASPHEMY", "ETERNAL DAMNATION", "JIHAD", etc to prevent scrutiny, if you are telling the truth why are you threatening people about it? The answer is simple: you do not want people to expose your gaffes and loopholes, period! Scrutiny is indeed the Achilles heel of twaddle.

The first sign of falsehood is its inability to stand-up to scrutiny and questioning. Whatever shields itself from questioning has a lot to hide. Religion forbids questioning and scrutiny and cannot stand-up to critical examination but at the same time it claims to be absolute, infallible and has all the answers. Isn't that an irony? Whatever that bans scrutiny, whatever hates questioning, whatever considers rational and critical examination as a taboo must not be dignified to have Truth or answers. Religion uses threats and the fear factor to propagate its message while shielding itself from scrutiny. Those who scrutinize and ask questions are considered devils, sinners and all forms senseless adjectives. The real devil and sinner is the religion, for whatever is righteous fears not questioning and rational examination. Every great assertion must stand up to great questions.

That which refuses to answer questions should not be allowed to make claims. Once your ideology is offended by questioning, it is offensive for it to claim answers. I do not trust anything that does not want me to question him/her/it and at the same time it claims to offer me truth and answers.

TRUTH IS:
- Answerable to questions
- Does not shy away from scrutiny
- It is not insolent at investigations

- Tolerates quizzing and shakes hand with evidence
- It is no foe with ridicule. In short, she is a Siamese twin with ridicule. When truth visits falsehood, she is called "ridicule". When she knocks on the door of lies, she is called "blasphemy".

Does your venerated ideology tolerate scrutiny? Is she an enemy with questioning? Does she shake-hands with evidence? When she hears a knock on her door, does she scream "blasphemy!"? If she is guilty in the court above, be kind enough to strip her naked and do not call her truth; that is an identity theft. It only makes you an accomplice when you shield her from Justice from the court of "R"- Reason, Reality and Rationality.

If you are still hiding her in your home; bring the criminal out let's stone her to death.

Contrary to the popular line that: "The Truth is bitter". I do not think so. Truth is covered in innocence and has no necessary affiliation with the kingdom of taste. It is neither sweet, soar nor bitter. It is only received in bitterness by those living a lie. Truth is blind to feelings; it is neither hurtful nor comforting. Those who are not favoured by her find her hurtful. She is chaste, celibate, independent, neither having a slave nor master, neither corrupt or of contumacy. It is when falsehood is the despot in authority that she is accused of contumacy. Truth is not a function of numbers or mass patronage. She is what she is irrespective of the numbers of patronizing her.

"Whatever that is asserted without evidence should be dismissed without evidence"- Christopher Hitchens

In religion, there is always a curse and threat to every assertion declared alongside the false promises and pious hope. For example in Islam whoever does not recognize and accept Prophet Mohammed as the last messenger and servant of Allah will be tortured in hell. In Christianity, whoever does not accept Jesus as Lord and Son of God will be condemned to hell. Why are they threatening people? Does anyone need threats to know the sun and the moon is real? Just imagine this: what would you make of me if I go about saying "anyone who doesn't accept that I am Imoh David aka Son of David, such a person is fool, idiot, and would be burned in a celestial oven underground"? First of all, if I am truly the name I answer, why would I go about threatening people to accept my name? Do you need threats to know that you're reading a book or there exist a company called NOKIA?

Say God exists and he has a religion. It'll be justified if he'll help make us certain about his existence and what religion and exact beliefs he wants us to adhere to. Then if we don't, he may punish us. But punishing people who are uncertain about his existence or exactly what he wants isn't fair. The contradiction among/within religions and people who sincerely claim absolute truth concerning God and what he wants (if any) is too much. This is a problem. Nobody doubts that the Sun is in the sky.

WHO IS AND WHAT IS GOD?

God (real or not real) is a BEING. What is a Being? A being is whatever that exists, whatever has REALITY, ENTITY, FORM, NATURE, or PERSONA. It is either physical (goat, car, stone, etc), mathematical or scientific (triangle, gravity, quantum theory, BODMAS etc), biological (DNA, nucleus, chromosomes, etc), chemical (oxygen, hydrogen, etc), intellectual, logical or philosophical (the human mind, thoughts, reasoning), even metaphysical or spiritual (sleep, dream, coma, etc). A Being can be potential or actual, visible or invisible (oxygen, bacteria,etc) dependent or independent. In other words, being has no real-time DEFINITION but rather DESCRIPTION.

That said, "BEING" cannot be satisfactorily defined but rather described or ascribed to a certain form, character, persona, notion, method, style, etc. But one thing is certain, whatever is called a BEING must be *per se notum* (Self-evident). Existence is a prime characteristic of a being. If it is not self evident then it cannot pass for a BEING. To some,

God is a "Necessary and Contingent being", meaning its non-existence is impossible, and its existence is independent of all conditions. Others say it is "Ontologically Absolute Being", meaning it can exist without reference to another being.

Arguments For The Existence Of God

A lot of schools of thoughts have emerged to argue for the existence of God, but I'll pick a few of them to analyze in brevity:

SPIRITUALISM: This theory was postulated by one Henri Bergson in his book "*LES DEUX SOURCES DE MORALE ET DE LA RELIGION (1932)*". According to him, the true knowledge of God's existence can be known through mystical and spiritual intuition that has a philosophical weight.

COMMON CONSENT (*Consensus Gentium*): This argues that almost all of mankind have the perception and agree that God exists even though they may differ in details, law, nature and postulation of what that God is really like. B. Boedder puts it this way "the universal consent of nations in the recognition of God must be deemed the voice of universal reason yielding evidence of truth".

RELIGIOUS CLAIMS: This argues that a lot of religious books has accounted the innumerable encounters of people with God via religious history e.g. Moses in the bible, Mohammed and the rest of other figures in religious books.

ARGUMENT FROM SCIENCES: this is of the argument that man, through science has discovered the intelligence in creation of nature which is only explainable by a supreme intelligent architect or maker as the originator, in other words, God.

THE ARGUMENT OF MOTION: *Quidquid Movateur Ab alio Movateur* (Whatever is moved, is moved by another). By observation, we know that a thing moves because it is moved by another thing. And there will be no movement at all if there was no initial point where the movement started. This will be a *regression ad infinitum* of motion which is impossible and untrue. In other words, the starting point of all movement, the first mover, and the *primum movens immobile* is GOD

FROM EFFICIENT CAUSALITY: Whatever is caused is caused by another. A thing is produced or caused by another, that another is caused by another, etc. Nothing can be efficient cause of itself. For the thing which causes another to exist is caused by another to exist, and the first efficient cause which is responsible for other causes is GOD.

God: the belief that there was nothing and nothing happened to nothing and then suddenly an all powerful, incredibly, intelligent, invisible, being magically came from nothing and then created everything from the nothing that was left from nothing.

ARGUMENTS AGAINST THE EXISTENCE OF GOD

So many schools of thoughts exist arguing against the existence of God, I'll bring up a few of them and discuss in brevity

EMPIRICISM: This theory not only denies the existence of God, but every other thing that is not physical, experimental, scientific and sensible. Francis Bacon, David Hume, George Berkeley, John Locke are among the popular proponents of this theory. They are of the view that "**only experiential knowledge is real and true knowledge**", hence only empirical existence is real existence. In other words the empiricist says "**unless I see it, experience it before it can be called real**".

AGNOSTICISM: Agnosticism is of the view that we cannot know with certainty whether or not God exists. Hume, Kant, Voltaire and Bertrand Russell are part of this school of thought. According to the agnostic, there is no sufficient reason to prove the existence of a supreme being or not. According to Kant, such a supreme being is in an unknowable realm, hence it is non-sensible.

ATHEISM: Atheism, unlike agnosticism firmly denies the existence of God. The three classifications of atheism:

Practical atheism which is professed by those who live as if there is no God, life after death, retribution, reward, and judgment.

Negative atheists are atheists by birth who neither have knowledge about God nor do not care either to acquire such.

Positive theoretical (In some cases, they are referred to as militant atheists): are the class of atheists who not only assert the non-existence of God but will go on further to elaborate the argument against theism:

Friedrich Nietzsche asserted that God is dead. In his view, although God existed but he is now dead and man is the new God who has climbed to the super-power status.

Karl Marx and Friedrich Engels asserted that God's existence is the opium of the people who hide in the mist of oppressions from capitalist powers of class struggle. Karl Marx and Engels went ahead to postulate that "God" must be killed for the people to be liberated from slavery of the ruling class.

For L. Feuerbach, it was not God who created man, for there was no such God. It was man who created God in man's image. He went ahead to argue that such *oppressive fabricandum* on man must be dismantled for man to be liberated.

J. Satre is of the view that God is an obnoxious nihilism of primitive mentality. That the modern man has researched on these primitive ideologies and he now lives dynamically without God. And there is no rational justifiable ground whatever for the exploited man who has come on age to accept the primitive god ideology.

DIVINE ATTRIBUTES

By finite reasoning and comprehension of the existence of God, some qualities and attributes has been generally accepted and awarded to God and said to be only and truly possible to be possessed by God, I highlight only a handful of them in brevity:

INFINTY: Infinity translates "limitless". God is limitless and his boundary is unquantifiable and unfathomable for the finite mathematical exactitude.

UNICITY: God is indivisible and unsubtractable. He is whole and complete in oneness, in other words *Ipsum Esse Subsistens* (Self- subsisting essence).

INCORPOREALITY: God is not composed of matter or substances of material measurement. To be material is to be composed of limitation hence finite which is not part of a divine attribute. In other words he is immaterial, cosmic and metaphysical.

IMMUTABILITY: As an *IPSUM ESSE SUBSISTENS*, God is perfect, devoid of mutation, influence, changeability. He is already Himself, infinite and indefectible

ETERNITY AND EVERLASTING: since he is infinite, he has no life span or expiration, hence he is existing outside the ambience of time, as defined by Aristotle as numerous *motus secundum prious et posterius* (measure of motion according to before and after). Everlasting means lasting forever and eternity means neither having beginning or end. Only God has this attribute

IMPASSIBILITY: This means God cannot suffer pain or emotional turmoil. Pain is a factor of the finite, hence imperfection. God is infinite and absolutely immutable so he cannot suffer pain or grieve.

UNCONFINEMENT: He is unrestricted to space, form, modus operandi, etc. Anything restricted to a form, race, law and space cannot be passed for a God. Restricting Him to a form and space or modus operandi equates to limiting him, including the logic of this writer and essay.

OMNIPRESENCE: since God cannot be confined to a space, he is omnipresence, meaning, he is everywhere and anywhere. Since he is limitless, and infinite, he is ubiquitous and unlimitedly available at all space.

OMNIPOTENCE: meaning God is all powerful and his strength knows no boundary. He can do all things and everything.

OMNISCIENCE: God is all knowing. If God is all powerful, infinite, indestructible, then he knows all things.

INFINITE AND ABOSLUTE TRUTH: Since God is all knowing, all powerful, self-sufficient, timeless and perfect then he is an embodiment of truth and truth is him and he is truth an absolutely devoid of fallacy and contradiction. If a finite being like man can conceive a little truth in some things then the infinite God should surpass this finite quality absolutely.

ABOSOLUTE GOODNESS: The highest good is divine goodness which is only an attribute of God. Good is perfection par excellence and such is only conceivable by God. From him all other goodness flows.

ATTRIBUTES OF GOD IN RELATION AND COMPARISON TO RELIGIOUS VIEWS

After examining the few divine attributes of God, the question which comes to mind goes: if these are the Attributes of God, how then can we find this infinite, perfect being? How can we truly ascertain the existence of this God who is, ageless, timeless, all knowing, perfect in works, goodness, power, etc? If you say he cannot be seen how then can we know he truly exists? If you say he cannot be objectified or measured, how then can we truly know he is not a creation of the human intelligentsia? As I ask these questions, I remember there are religious books and doctrines which say they have the answers and illustration of God, as such I went searching and made the comparison:

UNCONFINEMENT: I went through religious books like the bible and Qur'an they failed to perfectly paint this attribute of unconfinement with regards to God. For in the bible, God is confined as a lover of Jews, with preferential to the male gender, in other words, biased, gender jingoist and racial preference in nature and the Qur'an presents him in an Arabic lingua which was said to be sent directly from heaven. Confining God to a specific, language, race, and form has contradicted His attribute of UNCONFINEMENT.

INFINITE AND ABSOLUTE TRUTH: Religious books have been proven to be full of contradictions, fallacy, unscientific and fallen short of mathematical accuracy and exactitude, which has been enumerated over and over again, in other words that cannot be passed for an infinite or absolute truth. An example of an infinite truth and absolute truth is "GRAVITY", though we cannot see it physically as an object, we experience it and can prove it at all times on earth, simple, just throw an object up, it will come down, that is an absolute truth.

ABSOLUTE GOODNESS: It is said the highest form of good is divine good and from God flows other goodness. As a matter of fact, He is *IPSA BONITAS* (Goodness itself). But religious books and doctrines often portray God as a lover of war and an inspiration of bloodshed. Some even went ahead to narrate how he destroyed the entire earth and cities either by sending his protégé or some elemental destruction. Even sometimes he is said to be the reason and cause of deaths, famines and disasters. Can this pass for absolute Goodness? Absolutely No, that can't be God. You can't say he is absolutely good and also illustrate and enumerate accounts of bloodshed to him which amounts to contradiction; another attribute which is said is not of God.

UNICITY AND IMMUTABILITY: the attribute of unicity is one which asserts that God is indivisible, unsubtractable and as such he is whole in oneness. But when religious doctrines depict God as a trinity "Father, Son, and Spirit", this actually contradicts this unicity and oneness which is said to be a divine attribute. And immutability on the other hand translates to him being unchangeable, devoid of mutation and influence. But in religious doctrines and books, he is often depicted to have come in the form of man as in the case of Jesus Christ who was killed and which again contradicts

INDESTRUCTIBILITY as an attribute of God. Also, the laws of the Old Testament in the bible are changed in the New Testament, meaning God changed his mind or laws and as such he is mutable, which is still very contradictory.

ABSOLUTE BENEVOLENCE AND UNPROFITEERING: Since God is absolutely good, and benevolence and unprofiteering is part of goodness, then God is absolutely benevolent, selfless and non-profit seeking. Since he is infinite, he cannot desire coin or profit from the finite (man), which ultimately is His creation, and of course what possibly can man use to pay God? ***QUID QUID AGIT, AGIT PROMPTER FINEM*** (whatever acts, acts for an end), this is very applicable to the finite being, but the infinite cannot be subjected to a finite postulation as such when religious doctrines illustrate God as One who is seeking souls of men (the finite) and He'll destroy the ones that fail to abide by his laws. This actually contradicts this divine attribute, for it paints God as a businessman, and profit seeking entity. If he is responsible for creating man, why then should he be expecting profit from something that is incontestably his?

OMNIPOTENCE: Omnipotence is the attribute which describes God as all powerful and can do all things and religious books and doctrines ascribe to this. But if one should ask the religious person to prove this assertion e.g. can God square a circle? Or like some religious African folks will say "I save a God that can use an egg to break a palm kernel just to shame the stone". If this is true He can do these things, can anyone show it to us?

That is the million dollar question they can't solve. If you don't show us, how are we supposed to believe he is omnipotent? And this leaves one to ask, "are you really sure he is omnipotent as asserted?" If yes, how can we know for sure? How can we prove this attribute and other attributes are real?

Also, if God is OMNIPOTENT, can he kill himself? If he can kill himself then that means he is not everlasting or eternal. If he cannot kill himself, then he is he is not omnipotent.

We should not be quick to forget that in the Christian doctrine, Jesus who is also referred to as God was killed. And this is what prompted the Great Shaka Zulu to say "It is only the Whiteman that worships a God that can be killed".

MY CONCLUSION:

God is unknowable and ineffable for finite description. For it is erroneous to describe that which is immeasurable, unknowable, unseeable, untestable, unprovable, hence any individual, movement or organization trying to describe or has already described God is not only erroneous but insulting to the definition of an "INFINITE BEING". As such, any finite being, concept or material that attempt to describe the unfathomable, inter alia, God is a jargon jiggery-pokery and a fatuous gobbledygook. All religious texts and materials which claims "absolute truth" and "absolute knowledge" on the subject of God is nothing other than a legitimate misnomer of stupidity inspired from mental masturbation, a case of a primitive schizophrenia made manifest in documented ridicule. The beginning of the greatest conspiracies comes in the context of "ABSOLUTE KNOWLEDGE AND TRUTH OF GOD"; all are erroneous and ridiculous. People who hold convictions without evidence make absurdity an envious virtue. Believing something that is unseeable, unproveable, unreachable, untestable, inexperimentable reconciles the awe in delusion.

ALL religions are based on faith and not logic or prove. Anyone who claims that his religion is based on logic or verifiability for whatever reasons isn't being honest.

RELIGIOUS DICHOTOMY

Religion says there is a God up there but he is unknowable, immeasurable, unseeable, and unreachable because he is invisible and exists in a realm that is beyond the comprehension of the finite and yet they proclaim an absolute law and infallible knowledge about him. How the heck can you write and declare an absolute truth on something or someone which is unseeable, unreachable, unknowable and immeasurable and untestable? Are you on drugs? Any substantive truth must first and foremost be accessible to all for test and conduct of analysis, hypothesis, hence, conclusion on the subject in question. You say he is an infinite, as such he is beyond the comprehension of the finite, and yet you proclaim about him in finite language, finite articles, finite materials, finite laws and finite illustrations. And finally when a finite rationale confronts your ideology, you go frenzy screaming "blasphemy"! That is totally awesome in the 21st Century!

Religion is fat on claims and famished on evidence. Religious believers aren't seeking truth; they are looking for the illusory pot of gold at the end of the rainbow. Religion thrives among the needy and most gullible. Religion doesn't mix well with fact and reality. In short, they are pretty much strangers. Religion makes fantastic and magical claims because it does not have to bother bout proving them.

Science works well because it recognizes and accepts that wishes, hopes, prayers, allegiance and faith have absolutely no effect on reality. Science and facts are true whether or not it offends your religious beliefs, but religion is true whether or not it's true or proven wrong by facts.

Isn't it remarkable that almost everyone has the same religion as their parents? And it always just happens to be the true religion. Religion runs in families. If we were brought up in ancient Greece, we would all be worshiping Zeus and Apollo. If we had been born Vikings we would be worshiping Odin or Thor. Religion spreads through childhood indoctrination.

Upon critical examination of religious doctrines and assertions, an independent thinker and rational mind will agree that they are nothing but dogmas, ridiculous opinions, primitive rhetoric, illiterate babbles and all are founded by men whose mental status, cetris paribus in this age would be tagged with certain disorders.

Never has it been told or said that an animal, say a "Dog", had a divine encounter or special experience or revelation and was sent to save other dogs, hence making him a "SUPER-DOG", "PROPHET DOG", "Messiah-Dog", etc. Only but man the ultimate of all mammals and homo-sapiens that have declared so. Ever since time and events have been documented, mankind has seen frequently the continuous influx of acclaimed "SUPERMEN", "MESSIAH MEN", etc all acclaiming to save mankind with a so called DIVINE MESSAGE. Most popular of these SUPER-MEN in our time are Buddha, Jesus (the one of the Christian bible) and Mohammed

Buddha was born a Prince, and died a beggar.

Mohammed was born a beggar, and died a Prince.

Jesus remained obscure until many years after his death Hinduism which was not founded by one man is left out from the bunch.

The accounts of their lives and messages were written by their supposed followers and disciples and one similarity they all share in common is an omission of an account of a certain point in their lives. For nothing is stated about the life of Jesus from age 12-30. Mohammed disappeared into a cave. Buddha had a long escape into the desert. Nothing was known about their suddenly disappearance, all we know was that each of them suddenly showed up from nowhere and began propagating a new law.

This is not unsimilar to other popular religious icons like Moses and Paul. For the fugitive Moses disappeared into the land of Midian after committing murder in Egypt, no account was known of him only to suddenly return to Egypt with a message to "Let his people go". The same with the biblical Saul turned Paul who on his way to Damascus, disappears to the Arabia desert for a long time and returns to the Romans with a message. This kind of trend is equally repetitive in many legends and myths, where a hoi-polloi absconds to who knows where, only to return as a super-man, great sorcerer, warrior, prophet, etc. But nobody truly knows what happened to them.

Whether these tales and figures mentioned above are fables or myth, that is a discussion for another time, but it is quite tempting not to observe that they all claimed they had an encounter and they all vanished to a life of a recluse, they all returned alone and poor but not without a so called message.

While the accounts of Jesus never stated what happened to him during his disappearance or statements accredited to him about his encounter, Buddha who happens to be the most philosophical, less dogmatic and humble of them all, simply puts it this way that he got hold of the secret force of the universe and mastered it.

Mohammed speaks crudely of being visited by "an Angel Gabriel with a message from God"

Moses "beheld God"

Paul was "arrested by God". - (Modified and Borrowed from: "BOOK FOUR (LIBER ABA)" BY ALEISTER CROWLEY)

The conflicting disparity in their individual accounts is noted, but in their time these men were highly revered and were called spiritual, prophets, messiah, teachers, etc, but in this present age where medicine, science and education has paved the way for mankind into civilization, these men, assuming they exist; primitive rhetoric, illiterate babbles, among other names including their mental status, ceteris paribus in this age would be found analogous with certain disorders, for religion is the perfect cloak and subterfuge for people whose mental state, cetris paribus will be deem unstable on the stake of rational and clinical examination. Religion is the perfect escape from mental incarceration. It is the excuse people give themselves in order to exercise insanity.

Everything is to be feared about men who claim to hear or have heard a voice which others are disabled from participating equal audience.

The Abraham-Isaac saga as narrated in the Abrahamic texts is a repugnant scenario and highly sadistic in its arrogant defilement of morality and good ethics if played in the theatre of today's world. What would you make of a news, reported in the dailies about a man who absconded with his son to an unknown destination with a knife to slit the young lad's throat simply because he claims that a certain voice in his head commanded so? Will you erupt with a standing ovation upon hearing such news screaming: "FAITH! FAITH! OH FATHER OF FAITH"? But of course nothing is wrong about the tale of Abraham neither can we quiz his mental fettle so far his imaginary consigliere bears the name "God" because it is written in a book our parents and society programmed into our minds.

More is to be feared of men who sincerely claim and are certain they hear some imaginary voices than the wild beast. More than anything else, harm has been done on mankind by men who heard inaudible voices and were taken seriously by others.

More than 1500 years ago, the story is told of an Arabian man who claimed he not only heard a voice but had a physical visitation from an entity he called Angel Gabriel (In Arabic: Jibril or Jibrai). After returning from this acclaimed encounter in a cave, he came with a new vision and mission; to establish the tenets of his voice (which only him had access to). True to this, he ripped throats, enslaved men and did as he pleased. Whatever he was pleased with equally pleased the imaginary voice he heard and whatever angered him, angered his invisible employer. He passed away, but his legacy is still here threatening the peace of mankind; in Iraq, Pakistan, Mali, Nigeria, Somali, Afghanistan, and just about everywhere. Oh! Lest I forget, this voice of his was called Allah and he was his last true messenger (according to what he said the voice told him to tell us).

Should we question the mental status of this man? Hell no! It is blasphemy to do so because he claimed the voice that spoke to him told him to tell us that if we doubt his credibility or question his authority, not only are we deaf, dumb and foolish, but we must be killed. I love my head on my shoulder, so I pass. I equally agree that when an adult man marries the women whose husbands, fathers and tribesmen he slaughtered, keeps slaves and even marries a 9 year old girl, that he is a very sound and holy man. And it is definitely men of this esteemable character and feats that hear the voice of God. I also agree that when a man uses the sword to spread his ideology, destroy lives and properties, there is nothing absolutely wrong about him, even though he had invisible friends and enemies. Like one time he beat-up his invisible arch-enemy who is a ground troll and tied him to a pillar but his invisible boss later set the ground troll free:

"Narrated by Abu Hurarira: The Prophet once offered the prayer and said, 'Satan came in front of me and tried to interrupt my prayer, but Allah gave me an upper hand on him and I choked him. No doubt, I thought of tying him to one of the pillars of the mosque till you get up in the morning and see him. Then I remembered the statement of Prophet Solomon, 'My Lord! Bestow on me a kingdom such as shall not belong to any after me.' Then Allah made him (Satan) return his down (humiliated)." ----- Sahih Bukhari 2:22:301"

There is nothing wrong about the above tale and I agree that it is only a sane mind that is capable of such feat. I pledge corporation.

Men who sincerely hear inaudible voices are very dangerous especially if they hold the commands of their invisible friends in high esteem. Such people should be far away from those who do not possess the magic of their hearing senses. Once an individual is at peace and corporation with the voice of his imaginary friends, he is an awaiting tragedy to his genius loci; neither person nor property is safe. Far be me from men who befriend invisible voices. What if the voice in his head tells him to do to me as the Japanese do to Sushi? Won't it become headline news? "Man stabs man because God commanded him", it will say. Oh, my bad! Men have been constantly slaughtering other men because God asked them to; my short memory is at it again.

The leader of the dreaded Islamist group in Nigeria, Boko Haram by name Abubakar Shekau claimed that he had an encounter with Allah who told him to launch a Jihad on the Nigerian state and Western institutions. True to the desires of the voice that he claimed spoke to him, he has unleashed the will of his invisible friend on the visible environment. He once boasted that whatever Allah directs his group to do, they'll do just that, even if he says they such eat human beings. According to him, Allah had directed him to behead defaulters of Islam and they have been doing just that. History tells us that he is not the first to claim hearing and doing the will of this particular invisible entity.

If you sincerely hear an imaginary voice all the time or in a robust relationship with an invisible entity, it will be a great service to those of us who do not possess your kind of ears to check yourself into a medical facility. Be kind to mankind and your environment by submitting yourself to the psychiatrist to kill the voices in your head and break-up the relationship with your imaginary friend or boss.

Another thing I've learned is that: if your imaginary friend is called Allah, Yaweh, Holy Spirit, Angel, God, etc then it means you are a prophet, man of God or a spiritual person. But if your imaginary friend is called Bill, Okon, Linda, etc then you must be sick or possessed by demons. It is all a matter of what you name the imaginary voice in your head. But that is not all. If you say that there are no imaginary voices and entities like Allah, it will be declared with certainty that you are mad and then locked up in a mental hospital like the Nigerian Muslim Apostate and atheist, Mubarak Bala. Don't you just admire the awe of the 21st century? Men with imaginary friends run the lunatic asylum.

The story of Balaam and the talking donkey in the bible (Numbers 22: 28-30) is exemplary of this insanity:

If I saw and heard a talking donkey, I would have a psychologist check me out. It is far, far more probable given we don't have any instances of talking donkeys and many, many instances of crazy people, that I would be having some kind of mental issue. But since it was written in the bible, it is most definitely an act of God and the Balaam character is indeed excused for a stable man, even more stable than an unbeliever of this story. That is what religion is all about, excusing crazy people to be men of God and turning people's mental cases and imaginary voices to unshakeable truth and divinity. Religion can simply be called believing in someone's fairytales and illusions and the religious founders are simply crazy men who were able to convince and enforce upon people to gain their sympathy that it is okay to be delusionary, crazy and mad. They (the religious founders) are one of the few mental people that got away without clinical examination.

Why doesn't anyone ever conceive that Moses must have been on some hallucinogen before he experienced the burning bush? The same story a mentally ill man would narrate upon holding a pen is what people believe with unwavering doggedness. The embarrassment of sharing equal imaginations with a lunatic is no longer counted as a problem, but to reject such is to be found guilty of an expensive mental trip. Truly, with God all things are possible!

It is only in Israel that a snake will talk, fire will be burning in a bush but all the grasses are green, a big bearded man will use a rod to separate an ocean water, etc they are all true and from God. But if it the same story is narrated to have happened in a village in Africa, it is the devil's work. In religion, you'll get fantastic stories claiming that a man lived more than 700 years and that the Lord was very happy with him. Like what the hell? Is he a man or a tortoise?

When a man is acclaimed to walk on water in holy books, divide the red sea, etc. it is called miracle. But when a real life artiste like Chris Angel performs same feat, it is called Magic and Chris Angel is called a magician and mind freak, not a prophet or a messiah. The lesson to be learned here is that when God performs magic, it is called miracle. And what they term as a miracle of God are staged performances with religious banner. When this same act is staged in the America's Got Talent show or any other live performances, it is certainly the craft of mind illusion and magic performance of artistry. It is is all about what name a magician or an illusionist gives to his performances and the type of building it was done.

If the same stories in the holy books were to be written by J.K Rowlings and J.R.R. Tolkien, people will be certainly be sure that it is a work of beautiful fiction. The miracle in religion is how it makes a group of people to believe a lie and a work of fiction as true and infallible but when these same sets of people see a different lie and fiction unaligned to theirs, they are always quick and intelligent enough to recognize that it is a work of human imagination. I do not see how the works of religious literatures accredited to the likes of Moses, King David, Mohammed and others is any more remarkable than the works of J.K Rowlings. Jesus did not give any special advice and teachings that Dalai Lama, Rumi and Gandhi could not have given. The ascribed sermons of Jesus did not say anything breaking and brand new which ancient African proverbs and Chinese adages have not already said.

If J. K. Rowling was afforded the luxury to create a religious work and a tale of creationism, I assure you her ink will concoct something more impressive and seducing than the works accredited to men whose historical existence is nebulous. Is it because they (the religious) are opportune to live in the age and lifetime of J.K Rowlings and Tolkien that they are convinced their works of literature are not divinely inspired? Or is it because these writers did not make claims of some divine encounter and visitation from a celestial being? Perhaps if Rowlings and Tolkien lived in the Stone Age and dropped their Magnum opus works, people would have jumped behind them to label holy. Now I get it; when a piece of literature is composed by a vaguely known primitive character in the Middle-East, it is called a holy book. But when a writer whose biography and personality is well known concocts same, it is called a beautiful work of fiction and bestselling novel.

The Muslims will claim with certainty that an Angel Gabriel sent a message to Mohammed while the Christian will profess authoritatively that Jesus is the messiah of mankind and the Son of God. Both will debunk the other's claims and pick holes in their assertions and beliefs. But one thing is primarily common to the two; none of them have proofs to their claims. All of them are illogical and easily passed for a fairy tale by each party. If a Christian wants to know how ridiculous his belief sounds, he should ask the Muslim, and if the Muslim wants to know how senseless his doctrines are he should inquire the opinion of the Christian. They are both brilliant and critical when they scrutinize each other's beliefs, but the mystery is how they refuse to accept each other's submission of ridicule but expect the other to accept their literature claims without evidence.

If as a rational person you were to confront the religious with reason and concrete evidence, you'll find a great barrier in his mind and perception because such individual is merely holding up to his perceived truth out of religious ego (which is always bias) and not on any rational standing, and of course fear. Many religious people deep in their sub-consciousness detect the incongruity of their beliefs and inhumane doctrines and texts contained therein their holy books, but fear is the ultimate chain. But in some cases it is a clear case of mental fascism and intellectual dishonesty on the part of the religious.

The contradictions, lack of proof and conflicting thoughts has given rise to disorganizations in religious creeds. In Islam, there are about 73 sects. Their difference in ideologies and acclaimed truths has led to conflicting ideologies like the Shiites, Ahmadiyyas, Sunnis etc. Hence, the moderates, liberals and extremists. And Christianity has witnessed a mass exodus and mutation from Catholicism to Protestantism, Pentecostalism, Jehovah witness, Sabbathicals, and the list is endless.

Contrary to the message of hope, salvation and emancipation these supposed founders of religion have been attributed to bring to mankind; instead, they have brought us chaos, war, disharmony, hatred, ambiguity, dogmas, tears and fear. Above all, they have created an avenue for extorting and controlling people through organized institutions tied to their followership.

Over the years, it has been claimed that God speaks to a selected few even though we have no proof of this. It doesn't cease to baffle me, even when I was religious, but I continued to believe out of fear. I don't know if it is difficult for God (if he does exists and wants something from us), to reveal himself to all and stop the hide and seek game that has caused humanity to get confused and vulnerable to fear, conflicts, fraud and deceit. People have hurt themselves and others over centuries and are still doing so because of their religious beliefs which can be best explained as imaginary and delusionary. They say that one needs to have faith in what the holy books says; the so called holy books written by man who is a creature of an embarrassing reputation of untrustworthiness.

For the Skeptic, there's no good reason to believe, and if he doesn't, he gets threatened with an imaginary hell, no matter how good a life he lives. It doesn't make any sense. A Religious figure that is probably a fraud or is suffering from religious psychosis says or claims to do something extraordinary in the name of God and we should just believe without thorough proofs? The so-called miracles and prophesies claimed to be performed by these religious figures are largely not verifiable and if they happened, they are more probably an art of illusions. Absence of evidence is the nail on the coffin of all flamboyant religious claims. The world will be less insane when people learn to rely on reason, logic and verifiability before accepting expensive claims, which cost little or no wit to invent.

Man, by nature is cruel, greedy, and selfish and can go any length to satisfy his lust and self interest even at the demise of another. Through the birth of religion, man has found a better excuse and solace to exercise his subterfuge and barbarism, hence constituting a problem to himself, his environment, his neighbors and countrymen. Terrorism is just the term, but religion is the motivation and fuel, a simple text as this culled from the Koran has albeit man to cause terror to his neighbors and brothers:

"Oh ye who believe! Murder those of the disbelievers and let them find harshness in you." Al-Tawba, (Sura 9:123)

Empathy is lost among us, thanks to religion and its pious hope/wish, for she has inspired enmity and bitterness among us. One takes up arms and munitions to strike another down because he was told "God" commanded so, and he never for a day wonder why God hasn't done the dirty work Himself but will choose to use a mere mortal for a stooge? Is He (the Almighty powerful God) cripple or physically disabled to do the slaying Himself? Of course they won't ask because they were told not to question "God", in other words, their sense of reasoning and rationale is anchored in a script. As long as religion is among us, cruelty, hate and disaffection will continue to build tents in our hearts.

"Extraordinary claims require extraordinary evidence."-Carl Sagan

RELIGIOUS CLAIMS AND FALSE HOPES

"Existence as we know is full of sorrow. To mention one minor point: every man is a condemned criminal, only that he does not know the date of his execution. This is unpleasant for every man. Consequently every man does everything possible to postpone the date, and would sacrifice anything that he has if he could reverse the sentence."- Aliester Crowley.

All organized religion has promised its adherents some sort of gratification and reward. Death being man's ultimate fear was the quickest and easiest way for organized religions to tap into the vast advantage and credulity of man by making promises of eternal and everlasting life; for man has in his deepest desire to cheat death and live forever. Knowing that these promises are not feasible on earth, the organized religion was apt to masturbate the pious hope of men by further stressing that these promises are only viable after death. Organized religions especially the Abrahamic religions even went further to add some extra bonuses to these phantasms: in the case of Islam, the adherents are promised 72 virgins, knowing following well that the thoughts of sexual fantasy in paradise furnished by heavenly beauties is enough to arouse a high libido dickheaded man to find such fantasy quite idyllic. Without fantasy, religion has no companion.

Christianity on the other hand resorted to giving its patronizers an extra bonus of equanimity (no war, no tears, no sorrows, no sickness, no bills, etc) with an extra splendor of royalty like streets of gold, everyone with a crown and getting attended to by Angel servants, of course the biblical Jesus made mention of preparing a mansion. Since these organized religions knew it is impossible for their adherents to all be rich and successful on earth (another great fantasy of man), they came-up with false hopes and explanations such as "Blessed are the poor in spirit for theirs is the kingdom of God", "The meek shall inherit the earth", "It is easier for the camel to pass through the eye of the needle than a rich man to enter heaven", etc. To further satisfy the curiosity and insecurity of the adherents who may ask "why are unbelievers rich?" they said "I show mercy to whom I choose", "The Lord blesses whom He pleases", "..Time and chance happens to them all", etc. To gratify their hopelessness of not ever getting rich or successful, they said "... Rejoice for the kingdom of God is yours".

The very notion of gratifying bonanzas and bonuses of virgins, gold, mansions and palaces in some Disneyland in the sky or some unreachable realm that requires only belief to gain entry is highly insane. The idea that good deeds or a good character is not required as long as you believe reveals clearly that this is indeed nothing more than a recruiting tool for the credulous and the fearful. Is it not a good thing we know it is bunk and the worst kind of bunk? The Abrahamic God creates a man to be born in India as a Hindu but will roast him in his celestial oven for not believing in him. Has anyone ever heard anything so ludicrous?

Religion is masturbation gone public....... Religion ought to be treated fairly like masturbation; men ought to keep/practice them in the comfort of their homes/bedrooms. Once you take it outside, even those who masturbate and those who claim they don't would have problems with you. But the irony of religion is that everyone wants to be the right one jacking-off in public and at the same time they would frown at others who jack-off differently, those who refuse to jack-off and those who tell them to jack-off inside their comfort zones.

Nothing blinds a man's senses like his religious-ego. All religious people are firmly convinced of the superior excellence of the claims and hopes proffered by their religion, which mostly was traded to them from childhood indoctrination and geographical accident. If you ask both the Muslim and the Christian about the authencity and proof, that their faith is indeed not a buy-bull, there is more than an abundance evidence and raison d'etre to be provided by both sides of faithfuls raging from quotes in their perceived "HOLY BOOK" to pseudo-science, historical grounds (which is stilled pointed to the direction of their holy books and pseudo-history), population of their fellow faithfuls, quotes from famous people and just about anything they can lay their hands on. To them, this is what evidence sounds like.

If you ask each of them why they think of the other religion as a lesser truth to theirs, the reasons and evidence they'll provide will be impressive. The Christian will sight instances of "MIRACLES", SIGNS and WONDERS of different kinds which the Muslim counterpart cannot partake because he is yet to acknowledge the potency of the name of Jesus. The Muslim would want to claim that Jesus, who is called Isa in Islam, is a servant of Allah rather than a son of a God. He'll go about beating his chest to pseudo-sciences in the Koran which he'll want to claim as an ultimate scientific truth. The Christian will show him that in fact his pseudo-sciences aren't any science by exposing its gaffes. The Muslim too will point to the discrepancy in the bible and the Christian will return the favor to that of the Koran, even sighting that all terrorists are Muslims because of the several countless verses of violence and homicide in the Koran. The drama goes on and on. But unknown to them, their religious-ego naturally conceals from them what the other is seeing.

I have observed that when the Christian and Muslim are made to engage with each other intellectually, the Christian, in his bid to convince the Muslim and present a superior argument will quote from his bible and the Muslim does the same thing with his koran. However, none of them will find the lines and opinion of the other's holy book any reasonable and convincing. They both conceive in their hearts that the other is delusional and lost. What I do not quite understand is how they are unable to see in themselves and their beliefs what they find ludicrous about their Abrahamic counterpart. It is marvelous how they have somehow quarantine their senses from seeing what the other is submitting against their belief but they somehow expect the other to accept their argument drawn from their holy books.

We are all defined by religious ego which is definitely due to our fashioned obsession that our religion is superior to others. This superiority administered by religious ego is the bulwark of all social and religious conflicts and the blindfold on every religious adherent. This religious ego is often construed by whatever people make-out as the merits or TRUTH in their religion or belief and at the same time they debunk and merely play down on every demerit, lacuna and falsehood their religion is guilty of as inconsequential and lackluster.

Those who worshipped the Greek gods used to believe that they had the final answer back then and they had their own share of claims and hopes to offer to their patronizers. Those who worshipped Oduduwa used to think that their story of the creation was the ultimate. The highest level of human gullibility is the belief that your religion is the final answer to these original questions- who am I? Where did I come from? Where am I going? What made me? The arrogance of that assumption has no equal in human folly.

All these false hopes and fantasies were in perfect tandem for the oligarchy in those days who grafted these primitive manuscripts to keep the hoi-polloi under perfect subjection and mind control. To take away their minds from revolution and protest against the authority, the papacy in conjunction with the aristocrats invented these things to lure their subjects' minds from reality, from state matters as they get occupied with the illusions sold to them. Like Napoleon Bonaparte said "Religion is necessary to keep the poor from attacking the rich".

However, this is the 21st century, the age of information, where dogmas are questioned, where prove is the linesman for truth, but men still hold crave to these delusions, but to the elites and the political class it is a great tool for politicking and control. To the con-artiste of the 21st century, it is a great means of subterfuge, brain wash and wealth amass like Napoleon Bonaparte said "I am surrounded by priests who repeat incessantly that their kingdom is not of this world, and yet they lay their hands on everything they can get". To the men of violence, it is another tool and inspiration to terrorize others. And to those of us who can't help but question, reveal, and investigate, we are the FOOLS and the INFIDELS. Whoever came-up with the idea of religion should be given a standing ovation for successfully reducing Homo sapiens to Homo erectus ad retrogressio, with just a mere book.

"Prayer, in my opinion, is an act of doubt, not an act of faith, for if you truly trusted your God's plan, you won't be asking for anything"- Michael Sherlock

Prayers and Miracles

> "Everything has already been decided. It was known long ago what each person would be. So there's no use arguing with God about your destiny. The more words you speak, the less they mean. So why overdo it?"- Ecclesiastes 6: 10-11. (NLT)

Prayer is an act of fear and insecurity. It is an expression of distrust on the part of the religious and believer. If everything is already predetermined by God from the beginning why bother to pray? The believer's prayer is an act of faithlessness and distrust in the will of his/her God. I do hear some preachers say "you have to pray according to WILL OF GOD. If your prayers are not in line with the WILL OF GOD, they won't be answered". Hence, prayer is the act of trying to change God's plan. It is the belief that "I know God has a plan and a will, but I think mine would be much better". Prayer is an indirect way of saying: "God I know you have plan, but I do not trust it, I'm not sure about what you have to offer, but here is mine and you should stick to it even though you already have a plan which will still disrespect whatever I have in mind".

> "And this is the confidence that we have towards him, that if we ask ANYTHING according to his will he hears us"- 1 John 5:14 (ESV)

So they mean to tell me that it requires your prayers to bring the so called WILL OF GOD to pass? If it is the WILL OF GOD why then bother to pray about it? In other words, if you pray about a thing and it refuses to change it simply implies that it was the WILL OF GOD that he wouldn't answer your prayers and it was also the WILL OF GOD that the thing you prayed for should be the way it was. In conclusion, prayers are simply meaningless. It is an overrated soliloquy. It is a way of having a conversation with yourself by pretending you are talking to someone somewhere.

"WHATEVER you ask in my name, this I will do, that the father may be glorified in the Son." - John 14:13 (ESV)

The believers assert that we are all God's children. Do I need to talk to my father or ask something from my father in the name of my brother? "Daddy, please help me in the name of Imoh my brother."

If prayers really worked, the government would control it, the capitalists and large corporations would employ "prayer warriors". The CIA, FBI, MOSSAD, MI6, and the countless secret services will be raising prayer warriors and will jealously hoard them on the classified file. If prayers worked, there would be no need for nuclear weapons and other sophisticated destructive inventions because all what feuding nations will have to do will be to utter a few lies of request to the invisible man in the sky and their will is done. Epicurus puts it better on the efficacy of prayers: **"if gods listened to the prayers of men, all men would quickly have perished: for they are always praying for evil against one another"**.

There would be no amputees if prayer worked and we wouldn't have to produce medicines. Organized religions lay fat claims to miracles as a proof of their God's existence. If any religious preacher or any other person has the ability to heal (resurrecting is even too far), then why

54

can't they simply move from hospital to hospital? That's where those services are desperately needed, and that's where the genuine patients with genuine health records are. I always feel much lied to when I watch some characters claiming to heal some sick imposters in the church or in religious rallies, then they try to decorate the lie with some forged medical papers. Let these "healing ministers" of the world storm the hospitals and empty the emergency wards, who wouldn't love to see that? Apparently this God, who split the ocean in half and concerned himself with the most mundane aspects of man's life; and who by all objective parameters has taken to celestial exile, is still appearing and talking to people and performing miracles, but this time only in the heads of a selected few.

"It may be that ministers really think that their prayers do good and it may be that frogs imagine that their croaking brings spring"_ Robert Green Ingersoll

The fact is this: the probability of God answering the prayers of patients and sick people is directly proportional and related to the level of the healthcare system in that country. Compare the mortality rate in a religious country like Sierra Leone and its healthcare system to the mortality rate of a more irreligious country like Netherlands and its healthcare system.

During the Ebola outbreak in West Africa, Liberia's President called for national prayers and fasting; that all citizens should call on God's intervention, healing for the infected and forgiveness for the nation. Nigeria, Ghana and other West African nations were not left-out in the praying exercise; for that is their expertise. While they were busy engaging in oral frivolities, their infected citizens were dying. But when American doctors got infected by the virus, they were flown back home and injected with a serum and they survived. The serum, however not officially proven and accepted to be effective, but it worked faster than prayers. When the news was broke in the media that a serum was used to save the lives of the infected American doctors, a Nigerian preacher erupted with announcement that God has answered the prayers of his people. In the spirit of the breaking news of the serum, some other set of Africans whose art is in the field of blaming anything and everything on the West said the Virus was invented by the West to depopulate Africans and test new drugs. That is the difference between ignorance and knowledge; ignorance is very costly. Prayer is a big ignorance on the part of those who practice it. It is self-ridicule to pray when you should be using your mind to offer solutions and work hard with your hands. Frederick Douglass, an 18th century former slave recounted his own ordeal of prayers: "**I prayed for freedom for twenty years, but received no answer until I prayed with my legs**". Ignorant people pray while the knowledgeable work hard to invent and in most cases, control the ignorant ones. The fact is that the chances of God answering a man's prayers increase when the man's wealth and knowledge increases. Sometimes I think that ignorant people deserve everything they get. . .

I once watched a documentary on the hardship of some local people in Niger Republic. The documentary showed how the local farmers were lamenting about no sign of rainfall, hence famine. They kept praying all day for God to send them rain and water. If the farmers were rich people, they would have embarked on an irrigation project and alas, water will come and their prayers answered. The Somalian and Mali refugees are crying for food out of starvation while the Americans and the British are eating fat and donating funds through the United Nations, UNICEF and other bodies to help them. The fact is that the British and the Americans have more money than the Malians and

Somalians that is why God will feed the Americans fat and starve the poorer nations; the truth is bitter here. If God exists, I'm sure he willingly punishes the ignorance of those who engage in frivolities and rewards those who are in the business of putting their intellect to use. Life is hard, but it's harder when you are stupid and it's in its hardest ebb when you insist on being stupid. Religion makes life harder for the ignorant religious man.

Another case of classical inanity is when some Christians utter unintelligible words and call it "speaking-in-tongues". Yes of course it is highly crazy to spew words you do not understand to someone you cannot see. Who does that if not the insane? Can you translate what you are spewing? If a mad man utters just about the same trend of your lingua and you equally participate in same fashion that ordinarily makes the two of you birds of a feather. Religion is an excuse people give in other to exercise their ingrained absurdities in a fashionable manner.

In my toddler age, I think it was in my primary 5 which is the equivalent of America's 5th grade. Prophet Abraham, a preacher whose clientele my parents patronized then, on a certain evening as I remember vividly after doing what priests do when they visit homes that grease their palms and oil their feet with that one paper which God insatiably craves from the pocket of men, a young lad which I was, had something for the prophet to tender to the sky council.

Galloping in the traditional style of a young chap, I confronted him at the door as he was about to dust his feet with the brown envelop that bore the "happy paper" that pleases both Gods and men, gifted to him by my father. I asked with optimism that the man of God lay hands on me and call on God to make me earn the 1st position in my class as we were about to begin our first term exams the next morning.

True to my desire, he wasted no time in pouring his heart out to the heavens. His voice so loud that if God was asleep, he would be awaken with the "sherimamama kantadum" the man of God was thundering into the air. Now I am an adult, I understand the brief melodrama he displayed is the famous permissible absurdity in oral gibberish, called "speaking-in-tongues". Besides, I have come to understand that the package gifted by my father must have aroused such a vociferous passion in the man's prayer to his God, who is most effective when coin is involved. Just ask the pastorpreneur.

After the lengthy prayer, I was glad and of course so sure that God will grant as the prayer submitted. That prayer was too passionate and compelling for God to ignore, I thought. Soon after his leave, it dawn on my toddler mind that perhaps some other kid in my class could have prayed to God the same prayer and that I am not the only kid smart enough to embark on appealing to sky-daddy for an unequal academic progress. Like a typical child, turning to my parents to bail my suspicion, I asked: "If everyone prayed to God to take the 1st position in my class, who will God answer?" I am not sure of the reply I was given, my memory tape experiences some distortion here, but I'm sure it can never be anything close to reconciling satisfaction and reason into intercourse.

Did God make me take the 1st position? You may inquire. We honestly know the reputation of God in answering prayers; mine couldn't afford such immunity from his Omni-snobbery. Too bad the wailing of his priest was not convincing to his omnipotence and benevolence. Or perhaps the white-bearded genie was irritated by the gibberish the preacher was spitting into his celestial exile palace.

"Joshua must have prayed to God earlier". "There is a type of way he prayed to God to answer him", I struggled with my childish dissonance as I clutched the 10th position while looking enviously at Joshua who had what God refused to grant me. To bail my childish dissonance, Joshua was quizzed by this Son of David:

"How did you pray to God to take the 1st position?" "I did not pray, I read my books", he defended. "Then your Daddy or pastor prayed for you", I suspected aloud. "My Dad does not go to church and we do not have a church or a pastor", defended Joshua. It turned out that Joshua had a higher IQ than the rest of us and that was the God that answered his prayers above mine; "wishful thinking".

There are only two answers to a request which is what prayer is; a yes or a no. For most part, there is no invisible man in the celestial space as such, the answer to all prayers is a no. But it is indolent and highly unremorseful to tell the religious that sort of thing; they have high nauseating mental unbalance conjoined with a malevolent disposition to accept a disappointing reality and reflection. In order to deal kindly with their hallucinations I'll simply pander to their fashion by telling them that perhaps God is playing hard-to-get, keep your lips more busy. He probably needs more convincing and romantic utterances to woo his intervention.

God does not answer prayers. There is no old man in the sky that grants anyone's desires. Even if the entity's existence should be excused briefly, the probability of him answering prayers are relatively and directly proportional to one's hard work, skill, money, resources, opportunity, etc just to list a handful.

If three individuals say Mr. A, Mr. B, and Mr. C prayed to God for a car, say a Range Rover automobile valued at $70,000. If Mr. A has an annual income of $150,000, Mr. B an annual income of $5,000 and Mr. C $75,000; amongst these three praying men, which of them is likely to own the

Range Rover car? Mr. A will acquire it more easily than the other praying men. But Mr. C through savings can acquire the Range Rover but we cannot attest same for Mr. B. God will answer the prayers of Mr. A abruptly and it is not the imaginary sky genie we are talking here, but his income and savings is that God which granted his prayers. Assuming there is a fourth man Mr. D who does nothing, earns nothing but prays and fasts day and night, how will God answer his prayers? Perhaps he assumes some Range Rover will be delivered from the celestial courier to his doorsteps. Mr. D's prayer falls on deaf ears; he has no God. For the God who would have answered his prayers, is not in his possession and that God is called Money or Income.

This is what my religious African brothers are blind to. They pray all day and night, producing nothing and yet suffer greatly because they expect an invisible man in the sky to miraculous create luxury for them. This to me is the most terrible fantasy to befall anyone, be it a group or an individual. If America, the world's most powerful nation should go to war with my country, Nigeria; the most religious territory on earth. If America should pray to God for victory in war and Nigerians do same, who will God answer? Isn't it the one with the higher fire power? Perhaps if Japan, a largely irreligious nation should go to war against Nigeria, who will emerge the victor? Japan doesn't pray but Nigeria prays, who will be the one to suffer the colossal damage to defeat? Nigeria's fire power is inferior to that of the Japanese; we need no lengthy debate to know whose side the coin of victory will be.

If God hears not the prayers of the religious Nigerians and accord the largely irreligious Japanese military triumph over Nigeria, does it not show that God is on the side of the man whose abilities and resources will make his work easier? How can we truly say that God answers prayers when it is the resources of men that speak depending on how they are employed?

My country, Nigeria happens to be the most religious nation and I doubt if there is any group of people on earth that prays more than Nigerians. I like using my country, Nigeria as exemplary of the fruits of religion. If prayers worked, Nigeria would have been the greatest nation on earth. If the belief in God or the recitation of prayers had any meaningful and evidential benefit, it would have been seen in Nigeria or on Nigerians. Unless the believers and those who pray will tell me as quoted from the previous bible passages that it is not the WILL OF GOD to answer the prayers of NIGERIANS or it has already been decided that Nigerian was destined to be this way, as such, praying about it is as good as pouring water into a basket.

The amount of prayers uttered daily in my country is enough to bring God down. If prayer was an industry and an exportable commodity, the proceeds from the prayers in my country would have been enough to catapult her to the seat of the largest economy on earth. Prayer is so much of a national fascism that the Nigerian state particularly sponsors religious pilgrimage for her religious citizens to journey to Mecca and Jerusalem to pray yearly; an all expense government paid trip with cost running into billions. Such vain and shameful waste, for we are yet to see any positive increasing returns for such dissipation on frivolities, but rather, there is endemic corruption, crime, illiteracy, religious insurgency, children and women rights abuse and unemployment. It is vexing to see how a rich country like Nigeria is home to one of the poorest and under-developed educational institutions and the state will rather insist in a culture of misplaced priorities in chasing shadows by funding religious pilgrimages while its citizens are largely poor, unemployed and uneducated. Religion is a frustrating malison to those who mingle with her.

"Who can overestimate the progress of the world if all the money wasted in superstition could be used to elevate and civilize mankind?"- Robert G Ingersoll

Assuming the Nigerian government uses the amount of money they waste in funding religious pilgrimages on education, scientific research and job creation the benefits to be reaped cannot be over-emphasized. It will save her a lot from the many woes plaguing her.

According to Bill Flavell, "the sum of 43 billion US dollars was donated in 2006 by the six least religious countries in the world to the most most religious counties. These donations came from Japan, Sweden, Denmark, Norway, France and UK to Africa." "If prayer worked, wouldn't the aid be flowing the other direction?" Bill queried.

SIDE NOTE:

A Muslim lived right next door to an atheist. While he prayed five times a day and was constantly on his knees in communion with Allah, the atheist never even looked twice at a mosque.

The atheist's life was good, he had a well-paid job on ship with half a year off, a decent wife and was friends with one of neighbour's wives and his children were progressing well in life, whereas the Muslim's business strenuous and earnings not as good as he wished, three of his wives always complaining and his kids wouldn't give him the time of the day.

One day, deep in prayer as usual, he raised his eyes towards heaven and asked: "Oh Allah, I honour you several times every day, yet my neighbour, who doesn't even believe in you and certainly never prays, seems blessed with happiness, while I suffer. Why is this?"

A voice was heard from above:

"Because he doesn't bother me all the time!" ~ **Imtiaz Mahmood**

"I am surrounded by priests who repeat incessantly that their kingdom is not of this world, and yet they lay their hands on everything they can get"- Napoleon Bonaparte

PASTORPRENEURS and PULPITARIANS

Napoleon Bonaparte, the French military and political leader who lived in the 18th century did not spare to note in his famous quote "I am surrounded by priests who repeat incessantly that their kingdom is not this world and yet they lay hands on everything they can get". One can easily imagine that the practice of priestly gluttony did not begin in this age, and it is in fact an inherent character of the men in fancy robes who mount religious altars to insatiably crave for the luxury of coins and the pockets of the simpleton.

The pastorpreneur or pulpitarian is the man on the payroll of everyone's pocket in the church. He is the reason why the churchgoer can't put his mind off on "settling God". He is the reason why the churchgoer will work twice harder in order to bring his proceeds to God of which the pastorpreneur is impersonating in practice. Men of God they call them, but Gods of men they are, for whatever they lay claim to the sheeple as the dictates of God, such declaration is certainly of God and the sheeple won't and can't question. When the churchgoer says he pays his tithe to God, they are the Gods in whose possession the tithe safely lies. Their pocket- the church's offering, their bank account- the collective proceeds of men and the minds of men- their football pitches. None other but these men solely control the mentality and minds of men en masse. The mentality of a religitard is determined by the oral blunder of his pastor.

They are like software developers, whose input determines the output and behavioral outcome of the religitard and churchgoers. Insult the religitard and every other thing, but say no word about his pastorpreneur; he'll skin you alive.

To the shepple, he is blameless. Even in his glaring blemish and corruption, they see evil and hear nothing. True to this, the pastorpreneur lives like God; for who can blame God? The choir spinsters are for his delight, to do freely as he is pleased. Fishers of men like the holy book labels them, and true to the title, all he needs to do is simply point at the desired spinster(fish) and the kill is all to his indulgence in the bedroom. After all, he who works in the altar must eat from the altar. The pastorpreneur not only possesses the power to hack into the wallets and minds of men, he can equally hack in between the thighs of the religitard bandwagons on skirts. As a man, you just can't help but envy the pastorpreneur; all he's got to say is: "Thus says the Lord sister Grace, 'commit thy vessels of milk and flowery temple into the hands of the prophet, that he may come his bowels into thy wet abode", and boom! He is laid. Call it the work of the PIMPINGSTRY, sorry, the work of the ministry.

Not only are the wallets and purses of gullible men not safe around these men, the thighs and breasts of maidens are not spared from their avarice. Whether a bachelor or a married man, the pastorpreneur is a lustful man. It is said by the old quote that "power corrupts and absolute power corrupts absolutely". The priest is one who wields so much power over the minds of the people under the sound of his voice and followership. He is one who is highly revered, wielding the age old primitive book tagged "holy" and above all unquestionably sacrosanct to dictate to people the affairs of their minds, what ought to be and not ought to be. He is regarded as the servant of God, the voice of God, one who knows the affairs and dictates of God more than the rest of the clan. As such, his voice is that of God, his opinion is God's and his demands are God's. He is the voice of God and the "God of voice"; the man whose voice supersedes every other voice in the mind of the religious. He is the man whom the people have appointed to deceive them, the man whom men have permitted to lie to them, extort them and determine to them what ought to be and not be.

More gullible and susceptible to their greed are the desperate single women in the church; the single sisters whose desire is to hear the one over-rated statement of two brief words "I DO". In the Pentecostal churches where some preachers are referred to as "Prophets" (PROFTHEFTS); preachers who are believed to possess some special gifts to perform miracles and hear in real-time from God, these desperate singles are their favorite play-toys and objects of quick extortion. Since the prophet is regarded as one who speaks with God in real-time and possesses extra authority and power to do certain miracles like giving husbands, jobs, healing, wealth, etc. The contest to please this very pastorpreneur is trendy and politicking in the church. The coins and properties of men are his gifts without even calling. The stupidity of the ignoramus is his blessing which he will ride happily on with a smile to the bank. Those who possess no cash to gain his favor that will draw his miraculous intervention into their predicament; they often opt to payment in kind either by being dedicated workers in the church, domestic helpers at the preacher's house, not excluding the services of aiding the man in times of erection. When it comes to servicing the bedroom of the priest and attending to matters of his priestly erection, the gullible spinsters and female religitards are the ones who happily tend to his libido. Like the religious who always defend their gullibility and extortion by the preacher say: "If I give to the man of God, I am giving to God not a human being. Because the bible says "WHOEVER RECEIVES A PROPHET … SHALL RECEIVE A PROPHET'S REWARD….." The acclaimed holy book says "FOR WHOEVER SHALL GIVE YOU A CUP OF WATER TO DRINK IN MY NAME ……. HE SHALL NOT LOOSE HIS REWARD". As such, it should be defended that giving one's vagina to the priest and tending to his thirst in erection and libido is "giving unto God" and not the preacher.

No other day of the week gives the preacher so much joy like Sundays. He is on his highest ebb on these days. You can never find an unhappy pulpitarian on Sunday unless of course the turn-out in the Sunday service was disappointing or the church offering did not amount to what he had hoped for. Cetris paribus, the pulpitarian is the happiest on Sundays.

Standing tall and high on joy on the pulpit, the pulpitarian is often the finest to sing the popular church song "I AM HAPPY WHEN THEY SAY LET US GO TO THE HOUSE OF THE LORD". Every preacher is at orgasm when the lyric of this song from the psalms of David is sung aloud. And the preacher never fails to echo "IN THE PRESENCE OF GOD, THERE IS FULLNESS OF JOY". If you are the preacher, will you disagree? Standing shoulders-high like an alpha-male on the pulpit and overlooking his congregation, he sees the vibrating smile of his church members, the happiness and willingness by the sheeple to be fleeced by their shepherd. He sniffs the air and smells the gullibility of the people, he inhales deeply and drops a worship song that expresses his innate euphoria, and true to his vibe, the people about to make him richer join to the echo of his joy as he closes his eyes to picture his bank figures about to add some weight. To the gullible congregation, they are certain that he is in the spirit of worship.

The pulpitarian is a like a spoilt child; a baby that refuses to grow-up and an insatiable whore. He wants to be fed, he wants his needs to be everyone's, the one to be serviced and he wants his desire to be everyone's burden. All he does is demand, ask, and beg, and above all, he demands like it is his right to be given. He wants a new car; the congregation must find a way to bring it to his garage. He builds a new home, the congregation must be involved. He gives nothing to people but wants everyone to give him everything. The only thing he gives to the people are adrenaline triggering rhetoric and sermons all tailored towards how they should give to his purse, which he'll tag as "the church". Give, give and give is what their mouth is dripping with.

Like a spoilt child and an insatiable whore, those who give the most to his coffers are his favorite, whom he appoints special sits and titles in the congregation. The men whose pockets leak the most into his coffers, their homes his feet shall find an unending tourism. Pitiable are those who have nothing to contribute to his bank account, for they do not exist. They are ones whom the axe of "church discipline" and discrimination hangs around. More pitiable is the man whose home the preacher's feet knew but fate took away the one object which brought the preacher continually to his yard. Like a used snack, he shall be thrown into the dustbin of history.

Pastorpreneurs are among the worst ingrates ever. They dance around men who contribute copious sums to their "PIMPINGSTRY" and greet the meager members with a snob appeal. When the person who is in the habit of showering their coffers with money is ineffective or goes broke, they dump the individual and move on to another host. They are parasites, ingrates and con men. All they care about is their business and you just have to envy the way they call it: "the Work of God", "the ministry", etc. They are in the business of competing against each other. Pastor A versus Pastor B; who has more sheeple, who is richer, who drives better cars, whose wife is prettier and more expensive. Their competition is even taken outside the church business to schools and private jets ownership. And the religitards are applauding to the rat race as their incomes are fueling the luxurious sports of the priests.

Priests are men of avarice on fraudulent robes saddling the minds of gullible men to the abattoir, slaughtering every piece of sense and reason in them and with no intention to spare any pint of rationality in their souls. They are the merchants of superstitions, marketers of fairy-tales and the parasites of the coins of men. You need not wonder why the politicians are found with them. Be wary of them for they will take your money, rob your senses and drain every drop of rationality left in your soul and replace it with fear, bigotry, pious hope for superstitions and buffoonery. Your daughters are not safe with them; they will snoop into their panties. Your young boys will not be spared either. And their fiery lusty eyes will not be taken off from thy green fields. Look upon them like the fox; revere them like you would, the lion.

Nigeria is a country that boasts of some of "God's best generals". Some of these so called God's generals work so hard and are in constant demand for miracles by their flock that they have purchased private jets to improve their efficiency. Yet, not once has God used them or any number of millions of devoted Christians to separate our Siamese twins or grow the limbs of our amputees. When it comes to these types of cases, it appears that God prefers the miracle of medical science. Oh, and tithes and offerings.

Due to the love and high demand of miracles and in the believe sudden success and healing in by religious Africans, the pastorpreneurs are apt in their commercialization by introducing commercial oil, handkerchief, water, etc for healing, quick success and long life.

One of Nigeria's leading preachers, Pastor Enoch Adeboye is known for his story on how he travelled from Benin City to Lagos city (an approximately between 285 km to 309km of journey) on an empty car tank as a miracle by God who told him not to look at his fuel gauge till he arrived in Lagos. Besides the story being laughable, one may wonder how easily religious people are gullible to buy any story as long it is attributed as a miracle from God. Isn't it ridiculous that God does not make cars, but he chooses to make them drive with an empty fuel tank? Adeboye who is solely the witness to his claim should impress all of us if all his cars are driven without fuel and of course his private jet too. If he drives an empty fuel tank all the time and flies a completely empty airplane tank, then we'll be convinced rather than coming to give us a story where he is signatory as the only witness.

If everybody believes in a miracle to solve all human problems, I guess we won't have scientists that are finding pragmatic solutions to our problems. If those things are too hard or too big for your God to do then we can conclude that he is useless because he only gets glorified for useless miracles. Religious fanatics and leaders want people to switch off their own minds ignore reality and the evidence of things and blindly follow a holy book and their tales based upon "private revelation".

This same Adeboye wants to build a 3km by 3km church, valued to cost more than $225 million in Nigeria; a country where there is mass unemployment, poverty and illiteracy. The funny part is that he asked his congregation to contribute the money and the resources needed to build his business house aka church. What happened to praying to God to send down the money from heaven? If you asked these preachers, they'll tell you that their God owns all the wealth and money on earth, but isn't it ridiculous that a God who is attributed to be the creator of the universe and all life forms is suddenly incapable of building his own temple or church? He needs humans to use human money and resources to build him a place of worship; very convincing indeed.

These religious leaders; the PASTORPRENEURS, the PROPHTHEFTS, have a way of coming up with words of con to hoodwink their sheeple. They'll say things like "build the house of the Lord and the Lord will build your house"; if the Lord cannot build his own house by sending down his angels to the construction site, how on earth is he ever going to come build your own? I am looking for just one building on earth that was built by "The Lord". If these "Pastorpreneurs" are convinced that the God they call onto is real they should simply pray a prayer and money will come dropping from the heavens like the same Lord did with manna, or do they want to tell us that the only place manna is conceivable is in their holy books? After all, their holy book says "with God all things are possible", I wonder if the word "POSSIBLE", is exempted when it comes to their God building his own place of worship with his own hands? They are the preachers of FAITH; they should demonstrate this acclaimed FAITH by calling on the heavens to erect their structures and not be demanding money from their poor congregations to build their business empires for them. Of course we know that's not going to happen because God never builds houses, people build houses, they (the pulpitarians) can prove us all wrong by showing us when, where and how God builds houses.

After using people's hard earned money to build their business empires and con houses, they'll stand boisterously on the pulpit declaring "Thank you God for building your house, for no man did this but you", "I say this with all amount of humility, I owe no man nothing. It is only God that built his house and no one". The fact is that if no one went to church, these preachers wouldn't have had a dime, so they owe every member of their congregation thanks and gratitude for contributing their hard earned penny into their businesses.

Besides owning private jets, mansions and flashy cars, these pastorpreneurs are in a competition of owning private universities in Nigeria. Bishop Oyedepo owns two universities; Landmark and Covenant universities. A Catholic priest, Rev. fr. Edeh owns both Madonna and Caritas Universities. Below is the list of some of the private schools owned by these preachers and churches in Nigeria and a rough estimate of their fees:

BOWEN UNIVERSITY - 650,000 NAIRA (more than 4,000 US dollars)

COVENANT UNIVERSITY - 600,000 NAIRA (more than 3,500 dollars)

BENSON IDAHOSA UNIVERSITY - 500,000 NAIRA (more than 3,000 US dollars)

JABU UNIVERSITY - 450,000 NAIRA (more than 2,500 US dollars)

REDEEMERS UNIVERSITY - 450,000 NAIRA

AJAYI CROWTHER UNIVERSITY - 350,000 NAIRA (more than 2,000 dollars)

MADONNA UNIVERISTY - 350,000 NAIRA

However, the school fees vary depending on the course of study.
None of these churches or pastorpreneurs have built a free school for the poor to get educated. Bowen University is owned by the Baptist church of Nigeria, operated by Nigeria's Baptist convention. JABU is Joseph Ayo Babalola University owned by the Christ Apostolic church of Nigeria. Redeemers University is owned by Pastor Enoch Adeboye's Redeem Christian Church. Benson Idahosa University is owned by late Arch. Bishop Benson Idahosa but run by his wife who is equally a Bishop. The Ajayi Crowther University is owned by the Anglican church of Nigeria and many more of them are on the way.

All of these universities were built from the tithes and offerings of the common people in the church congregation, but they can't afford to send their children there. These schools are only affordable by the rich but the poor people who are the predominant followers of these preachers and contribute their sparse resources can't even afford to send their wards there and the preachers of course don't give a damn. If you ask them, they'll echo "I serve a rich God and my God has no business with poverty", are you not being rich because of the summation of the tithes and offerings of these poor people? If you see a man like Bill Gates who is a billionaire, you know he is a billionaire from Microsoft. The same goes to Oprah Winfrey, Warren Buffet and co; we know their source of wealth. But if a preacher is a millionaire or billionaire isn't it obvious that his source of wealth is from the offerings and moneys of his congregation? As such, any preacher which denies that he doesn't make money from his church or congregation and that his money is from "HEAVEN" is a liar and that makes him even more fraudulent. They have private jets, latest cars, latest electronic gadgets, latest dress codes, latest political connections, latest monies (from the tithes and offerings of the congregation) and everything latest. Yet they tell you not to yearn for worldly things.

Many of these pulpitarians are wealthier than 90% of their church members and followers. If the preacher is richer than more than half of his congregation and followers, it is very clear that the congregation enriches his pocket; as a matter of fact he milks them dry. The preacher needs the congregation more than the congregation needs him. One needs not wonder why pastors of small churches are not as rich as their mega churches counterpart, and they are even addressed by the Christian community as a "PASTOR OF A SMALL MINISTRY". A preacher is considered successful when he has an over-flowing congregation, followers and several branches, not because of his works or services to his community or the people. One needs not be told that a preacher is in for the money and wealth acquiring and not some spurious gospel.

As a matter fact, a preacher being rich is anti-Christ and anti-gospel. The biblical Jesus was very clear on this when one of the religious teachers sought to follow him enquired:

Mathew 8:19-20: Then one of the teachers of religious law said to him, "Teacher, I will follow you no matter where you go!" But Jesus said, "Foxes have dens to live in, and birds have nests, but I, the Son Of man, have no home of my own, not even a place to lay my head."

But today's preacher is an owner of many mansions and choice properties, contrary to the ways of the biblical Jesus. At another time in the bible, a rich man came to Jesus to enquire from him this is what happened:

Mark 10:17 "Good teacher, what should I do to get eternal life?"

After enumerating he has kept the kept the commandments and done the needful, Jesus told him there is something important he hasn't done yet:

Mark 10:21: looking at the man, Jesus felt genuine love for him. "There is still one thing you haven't done", he told him. "Go and sell all your possessions and give the money to the poor, and you will have treasure in heaven. Then come, follow me.

After the rich man left disappointingly because the request was difficult for him to concede to, Jesus said: **"It is easier for a camel to go through the eye of the needle than for a rich person to enter the Kingdom of God!"**

Dear pastorpreneurs, why are you all so passionate about acquiring the treasures on earth to neglect the ones in heaven? Why not sell your fancy cars, private jets and give all the tithes and offerings to the poor so that your treasures will mount up in heaven? The answer is simple: you do not believe that there is a heaven, not to mention a treasure in heaven, period! There is no set of beings more anti-Christ than the pastorpreneurs, for they flagrantly snub the teachings of the man they claim they are serving. They'll rather dodge preaching such bible verses and say things like "he became poor that we might be rich", "it is the will of God for us to prosper", etc. Religion is a tool that can be bent by the preachers and politicians to satisfy or excuse their selfish desires.

The religious apologist many often a time will argue that religion is pivoted in altruism and its sole aim is to promote a gratifying and honorable course. In very soft terms, this is very wishful and dishonest. Religion is the business of the priests, the profits of the men in house of altars, the earnings of pulpitarians and the blessings of politicians and those in power. If religion was not a means of aggrandizement or scheme of the men on robes of chicanery, then where comest their wealth and profit?

The Forbes list of the richest preachers on earth saw to it that 5 of Nigeria's preachers comfortably intimidated the contest of wealth of the pulpit, namely; David Oyedepo, Enoch Adeboye, Chris Onyahilome, Mathew Oshimolowo and T.B. Joshua. In a simple sense of economy, for a man to be wealthy or amass income, he must create wealth, he must engage in commerce or trade. Men like Bill Gates and Warren Buffet are wealthy because of their entrepreneurship in selling products of technology to the world. If one should ask, what is a priest selling to make the wealthiest list, if religion was not meant for subtle extortion?

The irony of this is that these men come from a country where the poverty index is catastrophic. A nation whose Human Development Index puts at 159 out of 177. I'm referring to a country where 70.8 per cent of the population are living on less than one dollar a day and 92.4 per cent on less than two dollars a day *(SOURCE: the UNICEF's Human Development Report, 2006).* For them to make the list, it simply means they run a system of commercialization in the name of religious establishments. Then the next question is who are their customers and target market? The answer is staring at you in the above index; the 70.8% of the poor population that live on less than one dollar in a day.

When people are poor and desperate, it is easier to convince them of any twaddle and sell them some superstition in a hope to emancipate them from their predicament. The reason why priests prosper in Africa and black communities is because the society is highly poor and superstitious and people are willing to believe it is more plausible to wake-up one morning and stumble on a huge bag of money on the street than to farm and harvest later on. It is a society where most people can believe that it is possible for the chicken to come before the egg.

If the preacher is richer than his entire congregation, questions should be asked, "Who is helping who here?" "Who is beneficial to whom?" "Who is the more profitable one here?" Of course the religious sheeple won't and can't ask such questions. Isn't it ironic that people like Dalai Lama and Rumi did not make the list? Dalai Lama and Rumi live in the part of the world with richer citizens compared to David Oyedepo, Enoch Adeboye and the likes. Why are they not as rich as them? Two answers: Dalai Lama and Rumi aren't milking people of their coin, and also, they live in the part of the world where people are more economically buoyant and mentally advanced to be made a sheep. Buddhist monks don't make richest or wealthiest list, it is always the Christian preachers. This explains why Buddhism would hardly appeal to the largely brain-washed African society.

If a pastorpreneur were to hold a crusade in a city like Port Harcourt, Nigeria, the money and crowd that will turn-out will be so great that he will be smiling to the bank the next day. But if he should hold the same crusade in a more populous and richer city like Tokyo, Japan, not only would he have few turn-outs, but he'll end up being in debts after so much tax and no offering. As a matter of fact the people who'll attend his gathering would be African residents in that city. Isn't it obvious that it is mentality problem from childhood indoctrination?

The most profitable place on earth anyone should be a preacher and pastorpreneur is China. China's population is over 1.351 billion, the largest of any country in the world. But in a religious country like Ghana, an upcoming pastorpreneur of a new and small church can be seen struggling with 10 to 25 members, but that won't be the case if it were to be in China which makes about 20% of the world's population. A small church in China would at least have between 3,000 to 25,000 members in a single church service. And a very large church like Nigeria's Winners Chapel of Bishop Oyedepo in Ota which boasts of about 300,000 worshipers in a single service, if it were to be converted to a Chinese version, it would be smiling between 3 million to 10 million worshipers per service.

The analysis is very interesting and could give an ambitious preacher a hard-on to go start up a Church in China. But sadly, China is one of the worst places any aspiring or an already established pastorpreneur would wish to establish a church; they will all go broke! Have you ever heard of a pastor Xi Chung or Prophet Lee Chang or a Bishop Feng Chi or even an Imam Zhang Wei or a Sheik Wang Xiu? It is an unlikely occurrence to stumble upon like the coincidence of stumbling upon black panthers mating at night. Even though their existence can be testified of, they are as many as the testimony of the existence of a Monk Oyedepo, Monk Adeboye, Monk Mensa, and Guru Imoh.

I have observed in my small world that the Abrahamic God nearly does not call the Chinese and Japanese, I'll tell you why. The reason why the acclaimed God that called the likes of Bishop Oyedepo, Pastor Adeboye of Nigeria, Bishop T.D Jakes, Joel Osteen and others would not call a Bishop Wang Chi or a Prophet Li Feng is because that imaginary God knows you cannot tell a Ying Jing that works in auto-company that some nebulous God made you cover a 247.6 km on an empty fuel tank of a car. Also, it is an exercise of farting into the wind to attempt to convince a Li Na, a female medical doctor that a Jewish sky-daddy impregnated a virgin (without a penis and a sperm) to give birth to his son (which is also himself), so that he'll sacrifice his son (himself) to his sky version so that he can forgive mankind of the sin he alone is responsible for convicting them. You just can't do that.

Sky-daddy knows that you cannot tell a Chinese factory worker that it is better to pray than to produce. Sky-daddy knows you cannot tell a Chinese banker and economist that you should pay your tithe and give large offering for a blessing to drop from the sky. Sky-daddy knows this, that's why he'll never call a Bishop Xi Tai to a so called ministry because the Chinese are bad markets.

But when sky-daddy looks around, he'll ask himself "who can I tell that I live in the sky?" He'll ask "who is more likely to believe that the Chicken came before the egg?" "Who is the perfect person that can believe that prayers move mountains?" He looks around and searches, then sees the likes of Paula White, T. D. Jakes, Robert Patterson, Adeboye, etc and screams EUREKA!

Unlike the Chinese who cannot be told that their ancestors were SINNERS, sky-daddy knows that the religious African needs very little effort to be convinced that not only his ancestors were sinners, but his future generations as well, and also he is cursed by God because of the imaginary sins of his ancestors, as such he'll have to spend his entire life on his knees pleading and begging Sky-daddy for a so called mercy and grace to be deserving of a heaven he can only partake after death.

Unlike the Chinese who laboured vigorously and applied pragmatism to become the world's second largest economy, sky-daddy knows the African believer wouldn't want such long labour and rigorous planning that involves thinking and policy making, sky-daddy opted for the African like the Nigerians, because he knows they'll buy the idea that they can pray to become the world's largest economy in 2025.

The Chinese have image nausea and sky-daddy knows this. The Chinese cannot fathom the image of some curly hair Jewish man with a European look as a son of God and saviour of mankind. Rather than subject his son (which is also himself) to ridicule and rejection, sky-daddy will opt for the religious African who is ever ready swallow this without resistance. God does not call the Chinese man.

> **"It is easier to fool people than to convince them they've been fooled"- Mark Twain**

MEN OF GOD OR GOD OF MEN?

God doesn't make any sound or speak! Another thing which cannot speak is the inanimate and the dead. Speaking is an attribute of man that explains why only humans will speak on behalf of God. To accept that a human heard from God is to sell oneself to another man's fantasy, lies and delusions. Knowing how fickle, unstable, conspiring, unreliable, treacherous man is, why would anyone believe a man who claims he is the only witness to the voice in his head which he attributes to God? Ask the schizophrenic he'll say the same thing. The only difference is that if your imaginary friend's name is Brad, you are sick, but if your imaginary friend's name is God or the Holy Spirit, you are man and child of God.

The beginning of the greatest con on earth began when men began allocating titles like "men of God" "servant of God" "Apostle", "Prophet", etc to themselves. There is no greater fraudulent name and title than one which is ascribed to the spokesman and representative of God. It is one title that has no real procedure and process to acquire. Anyone can wake up one morning and start answering the name "man of God". Unlike a professional name and title like a lawyer or doctor, if one poses as a quack or charlatan, he can be tested and investigated, his university records and degree will be demanded, and his registration in the Medical or legal practitioners associations would be looked into. But as for a title like "man of God", how can we ascertain? We are yet to truly settle the argument on the existence and reality of the God concept not to mention the credentials of a man of God.

Religion is the business of the priest; it has nothing to do with goodness, holiness or helping people. The tithes, offerings, the stupidity and fear of people are the profits of the priests. It is simply a profession aimed at exploiting the ignorant, fearful, desperate and weak. It involves using the fear of death, poverty, destruction through verses of the scriptures and the ability to use sharp wits to take charge of every event and opportunity the gullibility of people presents to you. The Priest tells you about God and what God wants because he knows God better than the rest of the people, but you have to simply believe in his church, his religion, his God and his holy scripture.

Religion is only beneficiary to the preacher and the politician. Men hide under the title of the man of God to commit the most heinous crimes on earth. People with schizophrenia tendencies can quickly opt into the man of God title and claim the voices they hear are from God to evade mental incarceration. It is even worse if a narcissist claims the title and gets on the loose. The popular Nigerian preacher Bishop David Oyedepo slapped a poor woman on camera because she said "I am a witch for Christ", and of course he got away with it because he lives in a religious and corrupt nation that has no respect for human rights and the rule of law. It is no shock that corruption accompanies religion. Besides the so called men of God using their influence to con people of their coin and resources, the religious leaders use their position to bully and oppress the poor and those under them.

During the Ebola virus outbreak in West Africa, the state government issued a ban on churches and other religious organizations from holding crusades and other mass rallies for public safety concerns after the first recorded case of the Ebola virus in Nigeria was announced to the public. The Lagos State government had to send a delegation to Nigeria's acclaimed miracle preacher, Prophet T. B. Joshua and begged him to not allow Ebola patients into the country. However, when Pastor Enoch. Adeboye who was about to host his church's annual convention was approached he refused and could not be contained by the government. Despite the government's solicitation on the preacher to call off the planned meeting, he refused, except that he announced that delegates from Liberia and Sierra Leone (where the Ebola virus was epidemic), are not allowed to attend the meeting in Nigeria. You don't have to blame him anyway, if the President of the country could kneel publicly before you for prayers, disregarding the order of the state is the least of things to worry yourself about. A foreigner in a saner clime of the world would be stunned by such crass theocratic malfeasance. It is not new in this part of the world for religious institutions to defy public and social rigmarole. It is a regular practice here that your night can be made terrible and neighborhood reckless because someone wants to preach the gospel and practice his religion will-nilly you are disturbed or not, and it is totally normal to do so. Once religion is involved, every other thing is inconsequential and subordination is expected, even from the state. Welcome to my religious clime; Here, God of men sorry men of God are the arbiters of your sanity. Don't tell them I said this; they'll have my head for this, please.

The men of god seem to be obsessed with power and influence. The case of the South African preacher Lesego Daniel who made his congregation eat grass is an example of the obsessive compulsion to oppress which is found in many religious leaders and the free gift of stupidity from religion. To imagine that an adult human can willingly choose to partake in an act peculiar to ruminant species is beyond me. With religion, there is no limitation to the imagination of the craft of absurdity. Truly, the Lord is a Shepherd. This reminds me of the words of Charles Bukowski: "I had noticed that both in the very poor and very rich extremes of society the mad were often allowed to mingle freely." People ate grass because they claim it makes them closer to God as their preacher commander.

Just when I thought I've seen it all when it comes to religious absurdity, South African Penuel Mnguni of End Times Disciples Ministries Church commanded his members to eat snake and of course they ate it. Speechless, I am.

They (the men of God) have come up with schemes to threaten their congregations and sown seeds of fear and superstitions in them that there is some kind of punishment from God if they disobey them. They quote verses from their holy books such as "touch not my anointing", "believe the prophet and you shall prosper", etc. A certain Rev King in Nigeria was known for making his followers use his name for their surnames but such fashion of mental fascism for his name was not satisfying to him. He had a special whip which served the purpose of flogging his church members (including married couples) who erred. One day he evolved in his totalitarianism to setting some of his erring members ablaze with fire.

It baffles me that these preachers who constantly boast about miracles and the power of God daily, move around with dozens of security details, bodyguards and police escorts. What happened to protection from angels? If you hear them preach, they'll echo that their God is omnipotent and he'll send his angels to take charge of you and that you should FEAR not. Isn't moving around with an army of security escorts by a preacher of the gospel a sign of fear and above all faithlessness? So their security details automatically translate to protection from angels and God? Besides, these people are in the business of selling heaven to people, telling them how beautiful and peaceful and prosperous the kingdom of heaven is and most importantly, it is only attendable in death. But they do not have any intention of putting themselves on the line of anything that will send them to heaven. They do not want to die and make heaven. Even in their prayers in churches, they'll be praying against death. Isn't death suppose to be a thing of joy and great embrace by one who believes he is going to make heaven? Why would one who claims to have a father in heaven consistently display no desire to be joined with the father? It is either they do not want to make heaven or they not believe in the existence of this heaven.

Most priests see themselves as more important than the ordinary or average man in his congregation. They are generally of the certainty that they ought not to be questioned while they want to give answers and question others. Their mentality is that they are answerable to no one but the non existing sky-daddy, but others ought to bow to them because they are emissaries of some sky-genie. The gratitude goes to the donkey-level intelligence script authored by iron age desert herders who created personages and imaginary offices for the most obsessive compulsive power hungry men to fit into.

More than any set of humans, 99% of priests possess all or a considerable amount of these traits: selfishness, narcissism, greed, dishonesty, totalitarianism, materialism, egotism, haughtiness, excessive pride, arrogance, boastfulness, wickedness, deceptiveness, philandering, high-libido, capitalism, impatience, lust, Machiavellianism, etc just to name a handful. None, I have found with an enviable character worthy of emulation. Whatever is wrong with my character, I always see excess of it in preachers, such that mine was made humble. Even so, more wary I am of folks who objectify and worship the so called preacher as a role model. Watch them closely, they are priests by social practice- materialistic, Machiavellian, greedy, bigoted. and anyone who loves property so much cannot love people

Religious leaders are hypnotic artistes. It's all theatrical. Pay attention to how they talk. Their words are in beats, in particular syllables and rhymes. They talk to excite and trigger emotions. Once emotions are hooked, reasoning goes out of the window. Once a believer has crossed into a psychedelic-like hypnotic trance, any crap will seem logical. There has never been a more effective tool for total mind-control invented than religion. God and religion is the best fantasy you can sell to a hungry and desperate man. A preacher preaching truth is like the politician preaching honesty.

All you need to be a successful Pentecostal preacher in the 21st century especially in the most religious parts of the world is this:

Read several motivational books especially by Zig Ziglar, Myles Munroe, etc. next, read books on strategy to manipulate and influence people's behavior towards you. Works on Jim Rohn, Carnegie, etc are good considerations for this.

Then get to the specifics on how to handle Christians in groups. Study the nature of church politics. TD Jakes, Joseph Prince, Creflo Dollar, etc come in handy here.

With the education done, next is to get how to practice the art of oral wordsmith. The art of deploying rhymes and alliteration of words even if they mean nothing, but who cares?

Learn catchy stuffs like: "your attitude is your altitude", "I life without Christ is full of crisis", "If you do not pay your tithe, your way will be tight", etc any other inanity you can lay hands on.

Learn how to emphasize on your members to pay their tithe and give big offerings known as SEEDS.

Then acquire an accent and speech signature. Learn from T.D Jakes style. If you know how to tune your voice and tone to exude hype on your congregation, then you're good to go.

Get a nice haircut; don't play with your suit and shoes. The classier they are, the more convincing you will push the congregation to put more offerings.

Learn to spot your potential sponsors- angel capital providers. These are well-to-do individuals either facing family crisis or the newly made rich who are still plagued by the fear of penury and economic doom. Let them know the importance of sponsoring the God of man, sorry man of God, as a sinequanon of securing their place of happiness and endless riches. Many of these people will be charmed to submit to your authority completely as their spiritual Godfather, Daddy-in-the-lord, etc. I'm sure you won't reject the generous offer of exploitation.

Finally, get the foot soldiers. The poorer members are willing to sweat and run errands in distributing the fliers, cleaning the churches, evangelism and many other domestic church works. They will be willingly to populate the choir and protocol departments.

Start your mass evangelism and programs with themes like:

"Set for Supernatural breakthrough", "The oil of Success", "Marked for difference", etc.

But if you are in a place like Africa or any third world religious nation where the belief in witchcraft and demonic powers are high, use themes like:

"That witch must DIE!!", "Conquering the forces of Satan", etc.

However, if your members are formally educated, and they are mostly university graduates, then you have to pick a more sophisticated theme like:

"Rhapsody of miracles", "Anointing for Excellence", etc. it must have something catchy for the young and ambitious to find appealing. You're good to go.

As people become more intelligent, they care less for preachers and more for teachers- H L Menchen

Preachers and Teachers

I live in the part of the world where there are more preachers (pastors and sheikhs/imams) than teachers, and the effects of this is palpable for all.

A preacher is one who tailors his words to suit a purpose; one who appeals to the emotions of people and exudes much of a melodrama in his audience. The teacher is one who arouses the curiosity and potentials in his student, listener and audience. Unlike the preacher whose aim is to "SOW" into his target (which could be good or bad) with an intention to reap from him, the teacher "SHOWS" his student; he awakes his true potentials and loosens his mind to a world and mentality of no boundaries and endless possibilities. But the preacher locks-up the mind of the individual, buries his potentials or redirects his potentials and skills to his selfish desires. The preacher sows the seeds of FEAR and FICTION in people. The teacher teaches facts and arouses positive FIRE. The preacher works by scripts, he stage manages his sermons. The teacher is natural, real and unadulterated.

The preacher will FOOL you, the teacher will SCHOOL you.

Give the preacher a boy, he'll return a BEAST or a CLOWN; give a teacher a boy, he'll return to you a man, father and leader. The preacher converts a bold man to a terrorist while the teacher trains him into a leader, revolutionary/motivational persona or a skillful general. The preacher turns a humble/shy man to a slave; the teacher molds him into a philanthropist and a man of service.

If you have a $100, the preacher will come up with schemes to take the money from you e.g. pay your tithe, sow a seed. But the teacher will encourage you to save or invest. When the preacher looks at an individual, he searches for profit, when the teacher looks at the same individual, he sees possibilities. The preacher turns a talent into a TERRORIST, the teacher turns a talent into a TECHNOCRAT. When the individual errs, the preacher PUNISHES and CURSES him, but the teacher disciplines, corrects and encourages him. The preacher THREATENs you, the teacher STRENGHTENs you.

The preacher raises sheep, goats and a variety of herds from his congregation while the teacher raises eagles, lions and wolves. The preacher raises problem-makers, nuisances while the teacher creates problem-solvers. The teacher is the "IRON that SHARPENS IRON"; the preacher is the RUST that corrupts iron.

The preacher wants to keep you permanently in his congregation; the teacher will send you forth and push you into the world. The preacher will make you a stagnant man; the teacher will make you a strong man. The preacher diminishes you while the teacher accomplishes you.

With the preacher there are no questionings, with the teacher questioning and critical thinking is compulsory. The preacher is always correct; the teacher will push you to find-out what is incorrect.

The preacher pollutes the mind, the teacher prepares the mind

A nation, an individual or group that listens to preachers and not teachers, that puts more value on preachers than teachers will reap the diminishing returns of the adverse effects of preachers.

Compare: the benefits of listening to say T.D Jakes/Pat Robertson to listening to Richard Dawkins and Albert Einstein

Compare: being raised and tutored under Pastor Lesego Daniel (the grass feeding South African preacher) to being raised or tutored by Martin Luther King jnr.

Compare: being raised and tutored by an Imam in Yemen/Osama Bin Laden to being raised and tutored by Nelson Mandela. Frederick Douglass/Malcolm X

Compare: Nigeria to Japan

THE RELIGITARD
Word Definition
RELIGITARD:
A religious person, someone who does not know that the sole purpose of religion is to scam you out of your hard earned money in exchange for telling you whatever you want to hear about what will happen after you die.

The Catholic Church (as one example) has profited for nearly two millennia and continues to profit financially by making one feel guilty for ones biological urges and begging for any amount of money at every service they offer globally, even offering 'indulgences' in the middle ages, which amounted to being able to sin as long as you paid them for it afterward. Is it pure coincidence that 'pray' and 'prey' are homonyms? How about 'prophet' and 'profit'? (Middle ages) Peon: "Father I need forgiveness, last night I raped a 10 year old boy." Priest: "Give me all your money and say two Hail Mary's and you will be forgiven, my son." Peon: "I don't have any money." Priest: "Give me all your livestock and say two Hail Mary's." Peon: "But my family will starve to death." Priest: "Then it's god's will. If you don't do this you'll roast in hell for all eternity!! 1eleventeen" --example of a religitard being taken advantage of by a priest ~ Urban Dictionary

Who is a "RELIGITARD"?
According to the Urban Dictionary: The term is used to describe a "religious-retard" who is closed minded to the views and opinions of others, and who also voices their own opinions as fact; whilst committing crimes against human intelligence in the name of religion.

The religitard is the active church participants, the so called BORN AGAINERS, the Muslim fundamentalist, the enthusiast Muslim scholar who takes every word in the Koran literally, who refuses to accept any fact, thought and opinion other than that of their religious view. The religitard is simply a person engulfed by religious fascism.

They are the active church workers, the lovers and worshipers of priests, etc. You know the type of folks who are religious to their mobile devices. They'll readily use wallpapers of Jesus, Mary, Moses and their favourite preachers or religious symbols like the cross, moon and star, religious banners, verses and flags. Their mobile ringtone is often religious tunes like the recitation of the Lord's prayers, the voice of their pastors and favorite religious figures or any of the religious mp3 audio.

The religitard is a closed-circuit headed religious person who has abandoned using his or her sense of reasoning. They are the folks who are toxic on religious inebriation. Expecting anything intelligent from folks of this nature is like expecting urine from a chicken. They are not found wanting in the four "SELF" syndromes: SELF-INDULGENCE, SELF-ABSORBED, SELF-SEEKING and SELF-RIGHTEOUSNESS.

If the religitard is a Christian, everything about this type of individual is a Me, I, Mine, My, etc. Utterances such as these are very typical of them: "everyone died in the accident but MY GOD saved me", "MY GOD has blessed me", "I AM BLESSED not lucky", "MY GOD has lifted ME above MY ENEMIES", "I AM a covenant child" "God has HONORED ME above my peers", etc.

The proper religitard is a self-appointed speaker of God, the mouthpiece of heaven and the self-acclaimed ambassador of heaven. Below are the characteristics and symptoms of a Religitard:

- **HYPOCRISY**. All religitards are hypocrites; you can't take howling away from the wolf. A typical female religitard will criticize the dress code, relationship and behavior of other females as IMMORAL, SINFUL, PROSTITUTING, etc but they are secretly getting laid by their pastors, choir leader or a married man/ brother in the church. The male religitard will be the first to speak against FORNICATION and PER-MARITAL sex; meanwhile he keeps a beehive of porn tapes at home or in his mobile.

- **SELF ACCLAIMED SPIRITUALITY.** The religitard is one that is avowed in their acclaimed spirituality. When it comes to matters of so called spiritual life and knowledge of God they are self-assertive in their robustness. All religitards claim they know their holy books very well, they claim hearing the voice of God or some Holy Spirit speaks to them. Nobody prays better than them; some take their prayerfulness to a nocturnal level. I register my condolence to anyone who shares the same dormitory, flat or apartment with this type of religitard; its either you co-operate with their spiritual warfare or you complain and become an agent of Satan. In my country Nigeria, they are every landlord's and co-tenant's nightmare, once you complain about their social nuisance, then it means you are a witch or wizard that is affected by their mid-night prayers in their religitard diagnosis. They are nuisances even to their fellow religious folks.

The Christian religitard is never lacking in their boast of some spiritual gift and I need not forget to mention that God knows them personally because they are so important to him and have established a special relationship with him which others are not privilege to. In Pentecostal churches you will always find them speaking in tongues; you cannot separate speaking in tongues from a Pentecostal religitard. You can see them waking up one morning to say "God spoke to me in the dream, that so and so lady is an agent of darkness", and boom! Anarchy comes knocking. The religitard is the one whom God reveals their future husband

and wife to in the dream. They are the ones who are shown in the dream that they are ones their bachelor pastor will marry. The religitard is one whom God shows a vision, gives a word of knowledge, prophecy and reveals future events to. The religitard must be a social nuisance to be complete.

- **SELF-RIGHTEOUSNESS.** First and foremost, the religitard is a BORN AGAIN CHRISTIAN or an upright Muslim who keeps to all the five pillars of Islam and obeys all the commandments in the Koran. A religitard is one who is always right in his/her faith, feelings, suspicion, and of course no one knows God and the holy books better than them. Their fellow Christians and Muslims know this about them. No one does it better than them, no one knows it better than them; no one is more right-standing like them except their pastors, Imams and sheiks (of course the Imams, pastors and sheiks are religitards lording over other religitards) . Their drive from self-righteousness has made them problem makers in social organizations, including the church. Whenever you hear of a fight, controversy or scandal in the church, it is definitely the handiwork of religitards.

- **MINISTRY/CALL SYNDROME.** Since a typical religitard is an active church participant and Muslim scholar, they are usually deluded with the "I-AM-DOING-MY-MINISTRY syndrome", "I-AM-ANSWERING-TO-THE-CALLING-OF-HOLY GHOST syndrome", "I AM SERVING Allah". The religitard is always on the conviction that they are commissioned with some kind of ministry from God. If a religitard is gifted with some kind of talent like singing, dancing, speaking, writing, playing instrumentals, and in the case of the Muslim religitard: great charisma, using weapons, making bombs and shooting guns, then that is all it takes for them to begin their self-ordained mission. They are always on the self-delusion that some holy spirit, God, Allah is calling them to use their talent for FISHING for Christ and promoting the gospel (in the case of the Christian). The Muslim counterpart is for the eradication of kafirs (unbelievers), the establishment of an Islamic state under the shariah law.

- **ANTI-INTELLIGENCE.** since these folks have readily abandoned the use of their intellect, it is inherent of them to dislike and display crass nausea against anything intelligent and intellectual in nature. When it comes to the IQ level of these folks, there is no contest at the bottom of the ladder for them. They hate intelligent people, one of the recounting utterances from their likes would be in this manner "Philosophy is meaningless", "Scientists are agents of darkness, "logic is nonsense", etc. When often confronted with a superior intellect and argument, they often respond saying "RUBBISH", "NONSENSE", "FOOL", etc you cannot expect decorum and rational discuss with these type of people. They are set of religious people that say some of the most stupid things ever. If you're an unbeliever, don't even bother engaging them in an intelligent debate, they use dumb-ass logic and foolish scientific claims to assuage their buffoonery for example: "Even science and scientists have proven that there is God and that the word of God is true", "Einstein used the bible to proof the law of relativity", "evolution has no scientific prove", "all scientific inventions and laws had earlier existed in the koran", "Any scientist that does not believe in Allah is not a true scientist", just to name a few.

The pastorpreneurs and religious leaders love these kinds in their sect; they are the foot soldiers of their business houses aka church, for their skills and talent is the oil that lubricates the business empires of pastorpreneurs. They are the ones the sponsors of terrorissm use to haunt their enemies. When the pastorpreneur sees these kinds of Christians, he is quick to convince and preach to them that they for a HIGHER PURPOSE or CALLING, and will give them some kind of prophecy that they'll be singing, dancing, playing instruments (depending on their skill and talent) in front of a large congregation, where the anointing of the holy ghost will spread like fire, and that "NATIONS SHALL SEEK THEM" (of course that is the topmost prayer point of every religitard). The Muslim religitard needs to be reminded of the reward of 72 virgins in a celestial palace awaiting him with a bit of recitation of violent verses in the Koran and then, the act of terrorism is committed.

You know the type of Christians that patronize religious stickers? That is definitely the religitard. It is impossible to find the entrance door of their homes blank or plain; there must be some religious emblem and sticker with a loud rhetoric saying something, like: "JESUS' HOME", "THE BLOOD OF JESUS", "I AM A WINNER", "REDEEM FAMILY", "MY YEAR OF HARVEST", etc, just to name a few.

Once you see the car of a religitard, the stickers on them will do the talking, as a matter of fact a religitard's car would have more than one sticker and religious emblems on it bearing phrases like "RELAX, JESUS IS IN CHARGE", "SHUT UP! ARE YOU GOD!?", "THE FOOL SAYS THERE IS NO GOD", "SUDDENLY! GOD DID IT", "JESUS IS ALIVE", etc. and in some cases quotes from verses in the holy books.

These kinds of folks are social terrorists both to their fellow believers and non-believers. They are the ones who lie for God and their pastors. So it's not surprising to hear them claim they went to heaven and hell and returned and had some encounter with God. They are the ones who always have dreams and revelations that so and so will happen or already happened. They are the ones who destroy social organizations, homes, marriages and even their religious institutions.

They are busy-bodies par-excellence, unstable people, and garrulous bandits for the lord. Willy-nilly; they must want to partake in religious activities. That is why you'll find them in the choir, ushering, protocol and prayer departments. If you come across any of them just RUN! I repeat, RUN! They are the types that lurk around the pages of unbelievers and the atheists on social media to threaten them with imaginary retribution and to defend God on behalf of God. They are the ones who come on people's social media space to detect to them what to write and say.

Another very common trend about them on the social media is that they are quick to distance themselves from being religious, and they may want to identify themselves as spiritual and loving but this is a part of their inherent hypocrisy and self-contradiction. They run around engaging their attention on any updates pertaining to religion and advertizing their empty verbose.

A lot of them are chronic liars, sociopaths and psychotic social terrorists, try as much as possible to avoid any social engagement/relationship with them, unless of course you are a religitard like them. The energy they carry with them is poisonous, infectious and communicable. Only religitards tolerate religitards. Do not say this Son of David right here did not warn you!

Religitards like other group of people have their categories. I have decided to classify the Christian religitard into sub-categories:

i.THE PASSIVE RELIGITARD: is one who is not actively engaged in religious activities. If he or she is a Christian, in some cases they may not belong to a particular church. However, in the typical nature of a religitard, they must have a certain pastor or religious leader they'll have affection and reverence for. The primary reason why these types of religitards do not have a particular church at the moment is mostly because they had a fight and quarrel in their previous church, so they left in anger and irritation. On Sundays if they are not in church, they are definitely playing Christian music and listening to the TBN or any other Christian cable channel. They are the types that buy sermons on CDS and DVDS, which they mostly play on Sundays. Some high-voltage passive religitards may habitually play sermons in their cars even though they do not actively participate in the church.

When you ask them "what church do you worship in?" They usually claim membership of the church of a preacher they admire the most, for example he can say "I am a member of the Redeem Church", but they have not been to the Redeem Church in ages. Sometimes these kinds of religitards are quick to explain:

"I am composed of different Fathers-in-the-Lord. I cannot really say that a particular Man of God is my mentor because God has used different SHEPHERDS to groom me in the spirit".

ii. THE ACTIVE RELIGITARD: if this kind of religitard does not work or participate actively in a church or church activities, he/she will feel empty and restless. But when it comes to the active religitard there are of kinds:

a. ACTIVE RELIGITARD BY DURESS- this kind is an active religitard by circumstances beyond his/her control or anticipation. Most religitards who fall under this category are mostly those who have lost their jobs or unemployed. Their longing to get themselves entangled with activities to keep their minds and body busy has driven them into the scoffers of the church which is always open for people who are willing to dissipate their vigor, talents and skills into the pastor's business. Their unemployment is the profit of the pastor, and many of them engage actively in church in the hope that the God will give them a job or the church can support them. Some even engage in the church actively as means of socializing and meeting people. When such individuals become employed, they usually abandon church work, and the pastors will be whining on the pulpit about how the devil have made them lost the penchant for church. Unknown the pastorpreneur who is venting his loss of a free labor, the individual actually never desired what he did; he was merely working in the church under duress.

b. ACTIVE RELIGITARD BY NATURAL COMPULSION: is one that exists by natural circumstances. This is particularly applicable to those whose parents are preachers and church owners or were adopted by the church. There is a popular observation that the offspring of pastors tend to bend towards indifference to religious activities and their lifestyle are somewhat secular and liberal. The children of many preachers tend to act this way because many of them are not enthusiastic about church work. So they tend to be active religitards under natural compulsion of birth and family/environmental upbringing. As such when some of them happen to experience a breath of freedom, independence and self-autonomy, they to bend towards their inward longing. As we know, the Christian folks usually blame this on the work of the devil.

c. ACTIVE RELIGITARD BY ARTIFICIAL CIRCUMSTANCES: occurs with individuals with individual who are happen to become religitards because of their personal goals/ desires or because of artificial influences like participating in church activities to gain favour from a superior and boss. Others become religitards because of their personal goals and desires; this is very common for the single women and spinsters in the third world nations where the woman is regarded as accomplished when she says "I do". In the religious third world nations, marriage is regarded as a do or dies affair. Spinsters in this category become active in church activities in the search of a spouse. Many of them think that by engaging vigorously in church activities like the choir and ushering, they'll be noted by the teaming male worshipers who may develop interest in them. This kind of drive is most often the reason of social anarchy in the church because people see themselves as competitors and commercial threats. In church departments like the ushering and choir which is predominantly occupied by the females, the anarchy and enmity is a well known occurrence. Many of the spinsters of this group are out for attention and attraction; as such they compete and fight themselves for it. In departments like the choir in the church, there is so much gossip, beefing and hating going on behind the scene. Everyone competes to be the lead singer, the praise and worship singer on Sundays. And these spinsters dress vehemently to be noticed and outshine their counterparts.

In churches where the congregation dances around the auditorium during the offering time, the competing religitards can be seen engaging in a subtle dancing competition. The best dressed sees an opportunity to flaunt her apparel, the good dancer would always want to show she has it in her and the sexy, curvy spinsters with sexy legs will wear a tight skirt with a matching high-heel shoes to show the congregation what they are made up of. The ladies with beautiful legs who are not talented in singing choose to be ushers which gives them the legitimacy to walk around the church with their high-heel shoes in display.

The men have a fair share of their guilt in this one. The male religitard who is a busy-body often loves to be seen as the pastoral protocol and fake body-guard. You know the type of dudes who wear suits trying to look like some Secret Service and Men In black around the pastor. You'll see them running around the pastor like they on some serious security patrol. Stuffs like this make them feel on top of the world. Some male religitards in the congregation who are seeking the attention of their female religitards are often the first to move-out when the pastopreneur raises a demand for some money aka seed. They saunter slowly with shoulders high so that the female religitards will know they have some papers in their wallet.

Also, they are usually in a quiet competition with each other especially if two or more male religitards have a mutual female religitard they are trying to take to bed. If the other religitard is having an upper hand over his competitor(s), the competitors will resort to passive hatred against the brother, thus the birth of church politicking and fights.

All religitards are insecure people, whether male or female. If a new member comes into the fold and seems to be outshining them, they'll start exhibiting their paranoia. Their insecurity is brought to the table when they are at loggerheads and in competition with themselves; this explains why the church is the place of social anarchy and religious Machiavellianism. Unless the pastor is highly feared only then can they be minimal conflicts, but even at that, conflicts still exists.

"A wise man proportions his beliefs based on evidence"_ David Hume

FAITH

Faith is a well-tailored phantasm; a celebrated efficacy of a starry-eyed mental orgasm. Mind you, it is different from "optimism". Faith is a self-inflicted hallucination, an exaggerated sloppy and inebriated optimism with no sight or sound. Faith is a perfect tranquilizer for an escapist from science, reason and reality. It is the lazy man's orgasm, consigliere, and of course aphrodisiac. Faith still remains the best mercenary for championing falsehood, the ultimate emissary of brainwash. One needs not to wonder why religious doctrines and bodies impede on their sheeple the burden of "Faith"

According to the biblical scripture, "faith is proof of things unseen". That's why I have faith in unicorns. I want unicorns to be real so badly. Faith and delusion are one in the same and have the same definition. Faith is a way of making a wish under a different guise. It's a way of insisting that your fantasies, hope, imaginations and dreams will magically come to being irrespective of the how improbable and farcical they may be.

"Faith is believing in something that you know isn't true." ~~~ Mark Twain.

Bertrand Russell says it best - "Where there is evidence, no one speaks of 'faith'.

It's Friday and you don't need faith to know its Friday because it's evidentially Friday. There is a difference between objective (shared across all rational individuals) and subjective (held by less than all) faith.

Subjective faith is blind.

Objective faith is based on experience.

For example:

OBJECTIVE:

The chair is solid. I have faith that when I sit down I will not hit the floor.

SUBJECTIVE:

I have faith that I will be the United States President.

The problem with subjective faith is that it may not be in accordance with indeterminate details of reality. That is the difference between faith (objective) in science and faith (subjective) in the supernatural. Unconditional faith is the first step in the commitment to ignorance, and that is what religion demands of an individual, sacrificing your grey-matter on the altar of phantasm

Faith means to believe in something that others are telling you without evidence and many facts to the contrary. Faith works for the unknown and the unknowable, it is implored by people who are comfortable in ineptitude and unable to come to terms with reality or accept that they are basking in the euphoria of the inane

Faith is not evidence, faith is not fact. If it were evidence or truth, it won't be called "FAITH"

It means: "trust me, I'm saying the truth, don't ask questions, don't ask for evidence just accept it and believe it without or not it is not in tandem with glaring evidence and reality." In order words, just be an idiot! Faith is a childish opinion, period!

I do hear Christians say that faith without work is death. They seem not to understand that terrorism is an act of faith. It is faith at work. The suicide bomber is a man of an unshakeable working faith. And such faith at work brings genocide.

"Science is about the facts regardless of belief; religion is about belief regardless of the facts"- Clay Lawrence

To choose faith over reason, to hang one's intuition on dogmas and superstitions over facts and evidence is to sell oneself to foolery, a conscious betrayal of intelligence and to divorce being human. People who choose unconditional faith over reason have lost their homo-sapien status.

"The word and works of God are quite clear, that women were meant to be wives or prostitutes- Martin Luther (1483-1546)

RELIGION AND WOMEN

"THIS WHOLE DELUSION OF THE EQUALITY OF WOMEN IS A BUNCH OF FOOLISHNESS. THERE'S NO SUCH THING"- Khalid Yasin

Institutionalized superstitions claim that women came forth through the ribs of the man. This, to me is one of the greatest coup d'état of a farcical ideology in the modern world. It is so much a blasphemy against nature and science which has shown to us the glaring in contradiction of this twaddle made sacrosanct in primitive documents.

Man comes from the abode of a woman. Men ought to worship women for all were born and will continually be so through them. If any object deserves the quintessential assertion of God, it ought to be the woman; for women are creators and givers of life, hence, God ought to be a SHE and not a HE. Well, that is a subject of discussion for another day.

That being said, ideologies, movements and organizations which tend to abhor, demean and demoralize the woman are criminal and blasphemous which ought to be fed to the gallows of Hades. Any ideology that is scared of women is satanic and repugnant, as such, the Abrahamic ideologies which puts the guilt on the woman as the reason for the fall of mankind, ought not to be forgiven for such sedition and libel against nature. Nature in all description is found worthy to be called MOTHER; the woman, the truth be told, if the world was ruled by women and men were the subordinates, we would have no wars and less bloody conflicts.

Religion which is a creation of the male alter-ego thrives in diminishing the female ego while feeding the male with an over-rated importance, hence stupidity. This is the reason why the male religitard is usually a female inquisitor, female moralist, female dress code/character adjudicator and anything female exterminator.

The alter-ego of men is exposed in religion when it dictates what it wants for women, deciding what is offensive to God and awarding God with the pronoun He/him. If God is a he and I am a he as well, then that classifies us into the same genre of sex. I know I am called a "he" because I have a penis, if God is a he like myself, it must mean he owns a penis. The only difference might be that he's is an "OMNI-PENIS", while mine is just a penis. I think it is fair to add "OMNI" to his penis, since man has irrevocably granted the "OMNI" prefix to everything of God's. It will be blasphemous to deny same to his penis.

If you read about God in the holy books, you will learn so much about the boisterous male chauvinism made manifest in the God character through religion. This male egotism is often betrayed in the iron-age dictates of God (which happens to be the alter-ego of misogynistic primitive men) against the female.

The foremost characteristic of the malicious male chauvinism is it's insecurity about women and its drive to subsequently kill and reduce to less than zero the value of a woman while on the other hand making great appraisals to masturbate the male ego over that of the female. The Judeo-Christian-Islamic God not only hates women, but displays a lot of insecurity about the woman. The worst cases of acrimony against women is found in religion; the Abrahamic religions specifically. While Islam through the Koran concocts many misogynistic verses and behavioral curriculum vitae including dress code and marriage code for women through the Shariah laws, it ignores entirely putting limelight on the men with bad characters. Its laws are deliberately made to enslave the woman, give the man a limitless permission to abuse the woman and then to regard the woman as an inconsequential toy in the eyes of men. The end results we have today in the Muslim breed are:

- demoralized women with low self-esteem

- Volcanic egomaniac male misogynists cum champions of morality, hence the Al Qaeda, Taliban, Boko Haram, ISIS, Al Shabab, etc just to name a few.

I'll share a few of these misogynistic conspiracies:

In the Islamic contents of misogynist texts:

Tirmidhi, 104: **"Women are your prisoners, treat them well, if necessary beat them but not severely..."**

Tafsir al-Qurtubi (vol. 17, p. 172), **"Women are like cows, horses, and camels, for all are ridden,"**

Bukhari, (1: 6: 301) **"Muhammad said the majority of women will go to hell because they are ungrateful to their husband."**

Bukhari, Volume 1, Book 2, Number 28: Narrated by Ibn Abbas, the the Prophet said; **"I looked at hell and the majority of its dwellers were women".**

Sunaan Abu Dawud, 3.29.3911: **"A house, a horse and a woman is an evil omen; a mat in a house is better than a barren woman..."**

Tabari 1:280: **"Allah said, 'it is my obligation to make Eve bleed once every month as she made this tree bleed. I must also make Eve stupid, although I created her intelligent.' Because Allah afflicted Eve, all of the women of this world menstruate and are stupid."**

Sahih Muslim, 26.5528, 5529: **If there is a bad luck in anything then it is horse, the abode and the woman....**

Sunan Ibn Majah, 3.1851: **Beat your wives if they commit sinful acts; women are captives of their husbands...**

Sunaan Abu Dawud, 11.2155: **Women, slaves and camels re the same; must seek Allah's refuge from all these.**

In the biblical texts- Timothy 2: 9-15

"I also want women to dress modestly, with decency and propriety, not with braided hair or gold or pearls or expensive clothes. But with good deeds, appropriate for women who profess to worship God.

A woman should learn in quietness and full submission. I do not permit a woman to teach or have authority over a man; she must be silent. For Adam was formed first, then Eve. And Adam was not the one deceived; it was the woman who was deceived and became sinner. But women will be saved through childbearing- if they continue in faith, love and holiness with propriety."

"As in all the congregations of the saints, women should remain silent in churches. They are not allowed to speak, but must be in submission, as the Law says. If they want to inquire about something, they should ask their own husbands at home; for it is disgraceful for a woman to speak in church"- 1 Corinthians 14:33-35.

Seeing the clearly written misogynistic texts in religious holy books, why would any woman want to subject herself to an ideology that insults her nature? Perhaps they do not find them insulting. When people's rationality is replaced with miserly creeds, their cognition has been compromised, which in turn makes their comprehension of things to be sabotaged. When this happens, the things which should naturally insult them are excused by their cognition and the things which should not ordinary be deemed offensive puts them into an irreconcilable paranoia. With religion, one can excuse and defend to death what insults and destroys him or her but will turn around and be offended by the one thing that truly respects him and wants to add value to his or her being.

I have met a handful of religious women, Christian women precisely, who claim to be feminists and born again Christians at the same time. I don't just get it. You say you're a feminist, woman rights activist and at the same time you profess being a BORN AGAIN CHRISTIAN. Like what the heck are you feminizing? That the bible should be re-written? Or Yahweh should correct himself and create both Adam and Eve from the dust at the same time? That it was not Eve that ate the apple? Or Yaweh's voodoo spell that women should suffer in childbearing and under the male misogynistic repression should be revoked? That the biblical God should rather send his daughter and not the son? Or perhaps Paul of Tarsus' essays inspired by the Holy Spirit should be re-inspired by the new age Holy Spirit? I do not know if there are any such people as Muslim feminists, but if they are, I won't be surprised. The beauty of universal diversity permits the laundering of all manners of "clowntocracy". A Christian feminist sounds as awesome a Jewish Nazist.

The authencity of the God ideology is made revealed by the things God is concerned with: the dress code of women, how women ought to speak, how women should behave in the presence of men, etc. Isn't ridiculous that of all things that should concern God, the affairs of women seems to irk his obsession the most?

God who chooses to write a book for mankind, in all his made-believe glory could not present a document that will and can deal with the most critical issues of mankind like curbing inflation, stopping natural disasters, preventing food crisis, checkmating disease outbreaks, etc. no, he has no clue about that. What piques his interest are the most sordid and irrelevant issues. Religion is clueless and it's only useful in oppressing another.

The society we live in devotes so much attention concerning itself with what is wrong with the woman and how women ought to act, what women ought to say and not say. Many times one will find them come up with quotes like "a beautiful girl with a bad character is like a pot of beans contaminated with sand". I am yet to find a quote that makes a figurative expression and comparison of a man with a bad character.

Turning on the radio in the part of the world I reside, most featured on air programs are always discussions about the woman: woman this, woman that and everything wrong about the woman; how the woman ought to submit to her husband, how the single lady ought to speak and act in other to attract a man, what the girl child ought to learn, the dos and don'ts of a female, etc.

The truth is that we ought to be more worried and concerned about men with bad characters than women with bad characters. Men with bad characters are portentous than women with bad characters. We give so much attention to witch-hunting women in the name of religion, morality and conservatism. While the men with bad characters breed and roam freely, enjoying the multiplier effect at ease.

We have more men with bad characters than women with bad characters, and men with bad characters on the loose is the bulwark of all calamities and conflicts on earth; ranging from religion, through politics to all enclaves of a genius loci. The bad and greedy polithiefcians (politicians), pastorprenuers, policemen, legislooters (legislators), etc are products of men with bad characters that haunt us. Then why do we spend so much time hunting women and creating an imaginary moral and social constitution for them?

Most of these male religitards are highly vast in ineptitude, mentally impoverish and to a great extent, insecure about the womanhood. Their insecurity is best expressed under the guise of religious concocted morality and conservatism whose trajectory is best aimed at the female.

It is reported that every year in Pakistan, over 100 people (most of them women) are known to be victims of acid attacks. The Acid Survivors Trust International (ASTI) estimates that approximately 1,500 acid attacks takes place globally each year. Domestic violence and physical abuse of women is very common in Muslim nations and many of them go unreported and without justice. One in three women in Kuwait is a domestic violence victim and the perpetrators are rarely arrested. One of the cases of Pakistan's acid attack is that of Zakia whose husband completed defaced her by pouring corrosive battery acid on her face. Zakia suffered seven years of domestic abuse in the hands of her husband until she finally summoned courage to divorce him. The unrepentant man attacked Zakia who is equally the mother of his kids outside the courthouse.

Another was the case of Irum Saeed in Pakistan who got her face burned by acid by a boy whose marriage proposal she rejected. Likewise, Kanwal Kayum who got the same acid treatment by a boy whom she rejected for marriage. Another, Shameem Akhter in Jang, Pakistan was raped by three boys who then threw acid on her. Others include: Zainab Bibi,Naila Farhat, Saira Liaqat, etc the list is just endless. These are all victims of a misogynist religious society; society which obstinately holds onto the tenets that women are lesser humans. Religion is the ultimate excuse misogynistic men require to abuse women.

Besides suffering domestic abuse, the girl child is a victim of pedophilia and child marriage. In many Muslim nations like in Saudi Arabia which has the highest number of child marriages in the Middle East there is no minimum age for marriage. Such conspiracy against the girl child in the 21st

century can only be excused through the rule of religious doctrines.

The case of one Razieh Ebrahimi in Iran, who was forced to marry at the age of 14, became a mother at 15 and killed her husband at 17 comes to my mind. In the words of Razieh Ebrahimi after being arrested "I didn't know who I am or what life is all about. My husband mistreated me. He used any excuse to insult me, even attacking me physically." She faces execution in Iran. Most of these domestic and women abuse go unreported and denied justice in the courts of these Islamic countries and here is a one of the reasons:

Abu Dawud 11, 2142: "**Narrated Umar Ibn al-Khattab:** The prophet (pbuh) said: A man will not be asked to why **he beat his wife.**"

In the Islamic court the rape victims are actually the ones who get punished over adultery. One may wonder: Why are rape victims often punished by Islamic courts as adulterers? This is the answer in summary:

Under Islamic law, rape can only be proven if the rapist confesses or if there are four male witnesses. A Woman who alleges rape without the benefit of the act being witnessed by four men, it is regarded that the woman is actually confessing to having sex. If the accused happens to be married, then it is considered to be adultery. Pakistani politician, Mohammed Khan Sherwani stated "**DNA test should not be used as evidence in rape cases.**"Religion must be kept out of the rule of law in order for justice to not suffer diarrhea.

Qur'an (2:282) - Establishes that a woman's testimony is worth only half that of a man's in court (there is no "he said/she said" gridlock in an Islamic court).

Qur'an (24:13) - "**Why did they not bring four witnesses of it? But as they have not brought witnesses they are liars before Allah.**"

Qur'an (2:223) - "**Your wives are as a tilth unto you; so approach your tilth when or how ye will...**" There is no such thing as rape in marriage, as a man is permitted unrestricted sexual access to his wives. With this kind of barbaric law and excusable abuse on women, how can Justice exist? This in fact is a conspiracy against women in Islam.

The truth is that the male religitard needs a character balance more than any woman on earth, because above everyone else, he is more likely to be a social disaster to himself, the woman and the society at large. Take a good look at the Taliban, Boko haram, ISIS and the fundamentalists; while they subject women to mental and social slavery as the upright demands of their holy books, claiming to establish the wishes of an imaginary character, they in turn become a menace and nuisance to the entire world.

The misogynistic male religitard often sweats in his pants when he contacts an independent, successful, intelligent and mentally emancipated female which usually gives a dissonance in his alter-ego, hence driving him to his area of expertise; swinging their imaginary moral rod at the woman. An example of this was demonstrated by the popular American televangelist, Pat Robertson who said: **"THE FEMINIST AGENDA IS NOT EQUAL RIGHTS FOR WOMEN. IT IS ABOUT A SOCIALIST, ANTI-FAMILY POLITICAL MOVEMENT THAT ENCOURAGES WOMEN TO LEAVE THEIR HUSBANDS, KILL THEIR CHILDREN, PRACTICE WITCHCRAFT, DESTROY CAPITALISM AND BECOME LESBIANS".**

Also, Sheikh Salah Al-luhaydan in Saudi Arabia warned women that driving will damage their pelvic and ovaries: "Physiological science and functional medicine studied this side and found that it automatically affects ovaries and rolls up the pelvis. This is why we find for women who continuously drive cars are born with clinical disorders of varying degrees", he said. Prior to the statement from the Saudi Sheikh, in Saudi Arabia, it was reportedly claimed that relaxing the ban on women to drive would cause both men and women to turn to homosexuality and pornography. This report was unanimously endorsed by all 150 members of the country's legislative council warning that allowing women to drive will breed the consequences of homosexuality, divorce, prostitution and pornography.

The modern day Christian may choose to deny misogynism in Christianity and in fact may sight instances of women's freedom in the church. In the practice of Pentecostal churches, women can be seen holding leadership positions and allowed to preach sermons contrary to the words of the bible and call for women's absolute submission by Apostles Paul, a man whose words and writings are believed to be divinely inspired by God. The orthodox churches like the Catholic Church are tenaciously holding on to the original doctrines and practice of systematic exclusion of women from positions of authority in the church. Very recently did the Anglican choose to join the modern practice of the Pentecostals by appointing female Bishops. However, this hasn't appeased a dime in the misogynistic history in the practice of the religion. As a matter of fact their attempt to reconcile their religious practice to modern civilization is exactly what the great literature icon Mark Twain pointed out in his work *"From Europe and Elsewhere and A Pen Warmed Up In Hell"*.

In the words of Mark Twain: *"The Christian Bible is a drug store. Its contents remain the same, but the medical practice changes."* Mark Twain continued: *"Not until far within our century was any considerable change in the practice introduced; and then mainly, or in effect only, in*

Great Britain and the United States. In other countries today, the patient either still takes the ancient treatment or does not call the physician at all. In the English-speaking countries the changes observable in our century were forced by that very thing just referred to as- the revolt of the patient against system; they were not projected by the physician. The patient fell to doctoring himself, and the physician's practice began to fall off...."

The practice of the modern church by pretending that the bible does not forbid the appointment of women into leadership positions of the church and in other instances, women run their own churches is nothing other than a flagrant disregard for the authority of their religion; the bible, which I understand was infallibly inspired by God as claimed. The practice of the church in the 21st century is nothing but a revolution against the imaginations of their God and in turn, they have forced God to comply with the sentiments of today's world, albeit the word of God remains the same.

"To the ecclesiastical physician of fifty years ago, his predecessor for eighteen centuries was a quack", said Mark Twain. In religion, adherents of the new age often resort in trying to update and shift aside from the practice of her predecessors. Each adherent of a new age is often convinced that the adherents of old were unprofessional and blind in their practices. This is like the days where human slavery was practiced openly. While the bible permits slavery, the human race evolved to the consciousness that it is evil. Over time, the Church stopped engaging in slave trade but the religious texts that excused slavery still remains and today, it sounds like such a thing a never existed in the practice of the church and even if you were to remind the Christian of this, he will readily debunk it as an act of ignorance on the part of his predecessors in understanding the bible. Intellectual dishonesty is a chief

virtue one has to possess to remain tied to religion. *"There were the texts; there was no mistaking their meaning; she was right, she was doing in this thing what the Bible had mapped for her to do."* Mark Twain continued, *"So unassailable was her position that in all the centuries she had no word to say against human slavery. Yet now at last, in our immediate day, we hear a Pope saying slave trading is wrong, and we see him sending an expedition to Africa to stop it. The texts remain; it is the practice that has changed. Why? Because the world corrected the Bible. The Church never corrects it; and also never fails to drop in at the tail of the procession- and take the credit of the correction...."*

What we are simply saying here is that; just because women are allowed to exercise authority and freedom in the modern day church and in some cases, own churches, it doesn't mean the bible permits such practice. The words of the bible are very clear with no vagueness on this one; that women are not to speak or exercise authority over men in the church. The modern church is simply disregarding the submission of its constitution because the world today has corrected her of her misogynistic feelings. But even at that, some churches are still obstinately holding onto the original practice, but it is just a matter of time before they bend into the demands of the modern human civilization. The same goes to same-sex marriages. The bible clearly condemns and specifically states that homosexuals are tenants in hell. In the Old Testament mosaic laws, they were to be stoned to death. But the church of today now permits and conducts same-sex marriages and some have gay preachers while others obstinately condemn them. It is just a matter of time before they change their tone. A hundred years from now, the Christians of the future will be condemning those of today and calling them ignorant just like the ones of today are of the opinion that their predecessors 150 years ago who engaged in slave trade were ignorant and crude in their religious practice.

A society is emancipated and civilized when its women are truly independent, educated and free from mental and social coercion. The poorest nations which are predominantly religious in nature have illiteracy rate towering very high among the women population and this is accompanied by low self-esteem due to religious bullying and indoctrination. Stronger women means stronger children, for unstable women cannot raise and tutor children into stable adulthood. And a strong woman does not patronize buy-bull and self-degrading doctrines in the name of religion. All Abrahamic religions are anti-women and women of substance do not buy into them.

There is no doubt whatsoever in my mind that if the Abrahamic God had a celestial wife, that wife of his will suffer so much abuse from his Omni-misogynism.

The character of the Abrahamic God (be it Allah, Yahweh or Jehovah) as illustrated in its literature is about the most terrible husband, man and spouse any woman can think of having an affair with. It is no surprise that the character is the longest bachelor to have existed and still existing. It is fair to call him an Omni-bachelor or Omni-single. Despite the fact that he has never been married to any female before, it amazes me how he concerns himself with dictating the ordeals of the institution of marriage, divorce, sex, rape and the conducts of women.

The Christian version beats me hollow: Father, Son and the Holy-ghost. How can there be a father and a son without a mother in the equation? The architects of this literature were very careful to save their sky character the embarrassing cost of running a celestial family and Omni-household. As such, like similar ancient myths which predated Christianity, where Gods were told to have had carnal affairs with mortal virgins like in Mithraism, the Greek mythology of Zeus impregnating different virgins who gave birth to the likes of Perseus and Dionysius, the Egyptian Osiris and Isis which begot Horus, etc the architects of the Christian version were inspired from this to equally make their God character out-source a baby-mama; Mary who was the wife of Joseph.

Sadly, their craft did not shield them from the embarrassment that God lusted after a mortal woman to give him an offspring. From the biblical account it can be briefly summed up that when God commits adultery with another man's wife, it is called "Overshadowing by the Holy-spirit."

If God could have a son then, it means he could have more sons and probably daughters and grand kids by now. Whatever drove him to father a son back then could equally make him have more children. But I'm sure the religious cannot imagine this. Because to them God only had one son in the bible and that is the end. You don't have to blame them for their confined imagination.

If God exists, it is an insult to say he has or had a son and even more terrifying of a blasphemy to accuse him of having this son through inseminating a mortal man's wife. It is a terrible embarrassment that an omnipotent God would willingly exercise influence over a man and impregnate his wife. And we seem to forget who commanded: "Thou shall not covet thy neighbor's wife".

A character who is attributed great enterprises and limitless creativity and power could not create a wife or woman for himself to impregnate but would rather stoop so low to engage in such a divine scandal with a mortal man's wife? This to me is the lowest form the God character has been reduced to.

To think that God came down to engage in the same scandal men are guilty of and which he punishes them for is an irredeemable ridicule. The notion that God impregnated a female mortal to give him a son is as awesome as the notion that a man went low to have a sexual encounter with an ant to give him an offspring. The good thing is that it is just a fiction. The bad thing is that men believe this to me a true life event.

There is no God, nay, one in the world, and she dwells in between the thighs of the woman. As such, the woman does not need any religion to survive or be inspired. No, she does not need anyone of them. The woman is naturally armed and endowed to Omni-sufficiency only if she is aware of this. The woman only needs education.

The totalitarian ideologies and religions always seek to conquer the woman. They come in all packages and forms. They will come in the guise of adversaries one to the other, in philosophy and politics. They will fight over difference about world history, global economics and religion. But they are gallantly united in one thing; their dread and scorn of the woman. Scratch beyond the surface and dig deeply to reveal their inherent abhorrence. Organized religions especially the Abrahamic ones have only one consistent ambition, irrespective of their overrated holiness and sermons of morality; the demoralization of the woman. The bible male religitard is high on prime and can't get beyond the infatuations of a holy faultless, eternally virgin mother he can overshadow because of his divine right to be the head. Also, his Koran frenzy counterpart, who admires the lifestyle of holy promiscuity of the Arab Prophet desires a mute hole he can cage, defile and toy with, worshiping him, eternally servile...to be kept at a wary distance; retrieved only for insemination and then tossed into cage.

They maybe mutual irreligious foes, basking with myriad philosophies, fantasies and ideals, but they are united in demoralizing the woman and they agree in principle that the place for the woman to function is the bedroom and the kitchen. To them, the male is the king and the crown, and the woman his object of play to be subjected to any use that catches his fancy. While they may shower you with their spurious praises and quickie attention in their holy books, you are of only one great importance; child-bearing.

Dear woman, they are one and the same. Do not be affected with the fancy names they award you: "Queen", " "Pearl", "Mother", "Gift", "Goddess", etc. it doesn't change the subject and sentiments about you. Whatever fancy name they bestow you will not add any special upliftment to you.

Look around you and judge. They are not adding any positive thing to the world. They cannot build any enviable kingdom and masterpiece on earth, so how can they make you a queen? They have been fighting wars and destroying monumental legacies, why won't they trample on you if you are a pearl? They cannot even receive science and facts with opens arms, how will they receive you if you are a gift? They see you as the crudest intelligence of a homosapien. They are simply emissaries of servitude. And to ensure the enslavement of your womanhood is their craft.

They do not know what "mother" means, except as breasts to be suckled and scorned. Their imaginations see mother and whore in same light. Why then should you bother patronizing verminous hogwash which glorifies in diminishing your true potentials?

Dear woman, if you wish to fly, unclip your wings from the holds of religion. Religion which is the chief emissary of misogynism has been the greatest stumbling block to women to mount and transcend.

ALL women of ALL races and class fight the same battle; the battle of SELF WORTH and religion will rob you of your self-worth. Don't let her win.

Professor Maryam Mirzakhani has become the first woman to win the Nobel Prize in Mathematics. Her achievement is indeed unprecedented. "This is a great honor. I will be happy if it encourages young female scientists and mathematicians," the Iranian born Mathematician said in a Stanford University news release. "I am sure there will be many more women winning this kind of award in coming years. With education, women will be afforded the liberty to achieve this type of feats and even greater ones, allowing them to fully exercise their intuition, freedom, talent and enterprise in all fields of endeavor. Religion is the surest way of stalling achievements like this. I salute this brilliant lady for her unprecedented achievement and for opening more doors for more women to achieve their goals.

"One would go mad if one took the bible seriously; but to take it seriously one must be already mad"- Aleister Crowley

---

Decoding the Anatomy of the Biblical God

God has a FACE: Exodus 33:11- **"Inside the Tent of Meeting, the Lord would speak to Moses FACE TO FACE, as a man speaks to his friend……."**

God has an ASS to sit on a throne: Psalm 47: 8- **"God reigns over the nations; God SITS on His holy throne."**

God has LEGS to walk: Gen 3:8- **"And they heard the sound of the Lord God WALKING in the garden in the cool of the day"**

God has a RIGHT-HAND: Exodus 15:6- **"Your RIGHT HAND, O Lord, has become glorious in power; Your RIGHT HAND, O Lord, has dashed the enemy in pieces"**

God has EYES: Chronicles 16:9 – **"For the EYES of the Lord run to and fro throughout the whole earth...."**

God has a HEART and feelings: David is described as a man after God's HEART- 1 Samuel 13:14: **"But now your dynasty must end, for the Lord has sought out a man after HIS OWN HEART....."** Also, in Acts 13:22- **"But God removed him from the kingship and replaced him with David, a man about whom God said, "David son of Jesse is a man after MY OWN HEART......"**

God has a BACK: "Moses saw the back of God. In Exodus 33: 21- 23: **"Then the Lord said, 'There is a place near me where you may stand on a rock. When my glory passes by, I will put you with my hand until I have passed by. Then I will remove MY HAND and you will see MY BACK; but MY FACE must not be seen."** For God to have a back then he must have a spinal cord as well. Also, this contradicts the earlier verse of the bible in exodus 33:11 where Moses is said to have spoke with God "face to face".

Other qualities of the biblical God include:

Isaiah 42:13 **"The Lord shall go forth as a mighty man, he shall stir up jealously like A MAN OF WAR: he shall CRY, yea roar; he shall prevail against his enemies.** Here God is not just affirmed as a man but a "Man of War", who exhibits emotions like crying and roaring. Exodus 15:3 of the bible speaks in unity with this: **"The Lord is a MAN of war: the Lord is his name.**

Contrary to the claim of omnipotence of the biblical God, there are things which he cannot do. Judges 1: 19 narrates one: **"And the Lord was with Judah; and he drave out the inhabitants of the mountains; BUT COULD NOT drive out the inhabitants of the valley, because they had chariots of iron."**

From the above biblical accounts there is indeed no doubt that the picturesque of the biblical God is analogous to that of a primate. His physique depiction reconciles with the anatomy of a homo sapien; bearing limbs, hands, eyes and even an ass to sit on a throne. His characteristic traits is reputable of a misogynistic, insecure, racial prejudiced, partial, unfair, violent, jealous, vengeful, erratic, contradictory, deceitful, ineffably egotistic, boastful, and a vainglorious sadist. The only known homo sapien that exhibits such traits is man and man alone! Hence the biblical God is a burlesque of man painting God in man's image.

"The moment we want to believe something, we suddenly see all the arguments for it, and become blind to the arguments against it"- George Bernard Shaw

Only Atheists Die

My attention has been drawn to a certain fatuous essay that has gone viral in the Nigerian/African social media ambience. The short essay lists a number of famous irreligious people whom they say died mysteriously, thus attributing their demise to their unbelief and punishment from "GOD". Here is what it reads:

BERNARD SHAW while smoking his cigarette, he puffed out some smoke into the air and said: 'God, that's for you.' He died at the age of 32 of LUNG CANCER in a horrible manner.

The man who built the Titanic.... After the construction of Titanic, a reporter asked him how safe the Titanic would be. With an ironic tone he said: 'Not even God can sink it'. The result: I think you all know what happened to the Titanic.

Marilyn Monroe (Actress). She was visited by Billy Graham during a presentation of a show. He said the Spirit of God had sent him to preach to her. After hearing what the Preacher had to say, she said: 'I don't need your God'. A week later, she was found dead in her apartment.

Bon Scott (Singer), the ex-vocalist of the AC/DC. On one of his 1979 songs he sang: 'Don't stop me; I'm going down all the way, down the highway to hell'. On the 19th of February 1980, Bon Scott was found dead, he had been choked by his own vomit.

Campinas (IN 2005) In Campinas, Brazil a group of friends, drunk, went to pick up a friend.....

The mother accompanied her to the car and was so worried about the drunkenness of her friends and she said to the daughter holding her hand, who was already seated in the car: 'My Daughter, Go With God And May He Protect You.' She responded: 'Only If He (God) Travels In The Trunk, Cause Inside Here.....It's Already Full '. Hours later, news came by that they had been involved in a fatal accident, everyone had died, and the car could not be recognized, but surprisingly, the trunk was intact. The police said there was no way the trunk could have remained intact. To their surprise, inside the trunk was a crate of eggs, none was broken.

Christine Hewitt (Jamaican Journalist and entertainer) said the Bible (Word of God) was the worst book ever written. In June 2006 she was found burnt beyond recognition in her motor vehicle.

John Lenon scoffed at Jesus and few weeks later he met death.

Many more important people have forgotten that there is no other name that was given so much authority as the name of God and they have paid dearly for their sins. Many have died, but only God appeared again, and is still alive & around.

The originator or doctor of such a doltish essay is unknown but was not surprising that my religious countrymen who are ever ready to be inebriated in farcical gusto on anything that tends to refurbish and pander their phantasm and reaffirm their dogmatic chimera were quick to scream "EUREKA!" Let me break it down for them and any other religious person to awake their goof.

"In Psychology, it is asserted that it becomes difficult to accept the truth when the lies told to you were exactly what you wanted to hear"- Unknown

First of all, death is inevitable, it is real and it will surely come irrespective of your title, echelon, or belief. We would have been convinced if religious people especially Christians lived forever. Let us do a little math: the world's atheist population and non-religious people as at 2010 was estimated to be 9.66%, in other words atheists are a minority. By simple mathematical probability, the probability of meeting an atheist is adversely slim even in a crowd of a million people; hence, the probability of a dead atheist in 1 million deaths is absolutely sparse mathematically. In Nigeria, according to WIN-Gallup International poll, the atheist population in Nigeria is just 1%. Assuming Nigeria's population is 150,000,000, 1% of this is 1,500,000. So do these religitards want to tell me that all the people who die daily in Nigeria are these 1,500,000 atheists? It is tomfoolery for anyone to credit death or an ill-fate on anyone as a so called retribution from God as a result of his/her unbelief.

All the people I've known that have died were believers and strict Christian adherents, as such, is their death equally as a result of their belief?

They mentioned the famous music icon John Lenon, who was an unbeliever, but they failed to narrate that John Lenon was assassinated by a Christian extremist who said he was doing the "work of Christ" by killing John Lenon.

Nigeria's famous preacher, Kumiyi lost his wife to death, Archbishop Benson Idahosa died in the middle of a healthy conversation with his visitors, A pastor in Akwa Ibom state, Nigeria, by name Pastor Justus died while he knelt down to pray on the church pulpit, a popular Rev Uma Ukpai lost his Kids in a car accident that fell into a river from the bridge, Late Prophet Ajanuku, Late Rev Danny Kirk, and the other countless unpopular believers, etc the list is endless. I am mentioning these people with no intention to mock them or their family, but to educate the ignorant religitards across the globe that death is no respecter of any man and mortality is real. If these things had happened to an atheist or unbeliever, they would have said it is "GOD'S WRATH". It is absolutely iniquitous and crass coquetry in archaic guff for anyone to attribute an ill-fate or death of anyone as a result of unbelief or belief in a deity. I tender my unreserved reverence to the dead and the families of the above mentioned names.

The life expectancy rate of Nigeria where 94% of its citizens believe in God is 53years and the life expectancy rate of a country like Japan where only 4% of its population is certain in the belief of the existence of God is 83years. They should be asking their God why an average Japanese lives longer than a Nigerian.

One is moved to assume that religion magnifies the negativity in people. It either makes the person vacuously lumpish or self-righteous which equates to legitimate wickedness, bad attitude and hateful of others who do not share in his/her buffoonery. As a matter of fact, statistics provided shows that the life expectancy of a religious country is relatively slim compared to irreligious and liberal nations and individuals.

Upon the breaking news of the death of the international preacher Myles Munroe by a ghastly plane crash, the religious community were bereaved by his death and even the non-religious felt his passing away. And many submitted their heartfelt condolence as "It is the will of God" and "a call to glory". Such is the vanity and sadness of life.

However, if we were to imagine such a tragic fate had befallen the likes of say, Sam Harris, Stephen Hawkins or Richard Dawkins, how would the response of such tragedy be received and responded by the religious community? A lot of them would have unsparingly hasten to assign the fatality to some wrath from their Sky-Janitor.

And even among their sky-colleagues, if say, Pope Francis should die from a plane crash, the set of religitards who are certain that the Pope is a fake emissary of their sky-landlord or an anti-Christ beast, will gladly assign the cause of such a fatality to their own version of sky-daddy, while those who see him as genuine would say "the Lord has taken his Saint."

I know of one who participated in the vendor of the popular text (above) where famous atheists or non-believers are listed to have died as a result of some their malevolent genie's anger against their anti-skydaddy rhetoric. When Myles Munroe (who is his icon of admiration) was announced to have died, his understanding of this very tragedy became the "will of God", "God gives and takes", "A call to glory", etc.

One can clearly see that religion makes people selective bigots and all round idiots, no wonder it was recently said that religious fundamentalism will soon

be classified as a mental illness. If as an adult a person haven't noticed that life comes with a gift of tragedy and joy and no man chooses the scene to which his tragedy will be played especially the one that relates to death, then you are over-ripe for a claptrap award.

If a person is driven by a selective condolence which views the demise of a preacher as a will of God (which is a good thing) and the demise or any unforseen predicament that befalls an irreligious man is the craftmanship of some wrath of God, then such an individual is a fundamentalist and should be assigned an asylum.

We were born to die one day and that day of death, a man sparsely have the power to determine its scenario. Your imaginary will and wrath of God is less than a fable of a lunatic. Life comes with the bonanza of death, and like criminals awaiting trial, we try to evade the day of our death whilst we struggle in vain, for it shall surely come. No wonder they console themselves with docile promises of eternal life; sweet it is, so is the imaginations of a sky-wonderland, keep dreaming. Once you have come to peace with the fact that we are but brief tenants on this planet, then you will embrace humanity with humility, love and peace while you hang around.

"Christianity was an epidemic rather than a religion. It appealed to fear, hysteria and ignorance. It spread across the Western world, not because it was true, but because humans are gullible and superstitious"- Collins Wilson

Sex Sells, But Fear Is The Superior Salesman

99% percent of all suffering, anxiety, fear, and guilt are caused by something that is not even real. The cause is similar to a child who is afraid of monsters under his bed, and then when he looks and sees nothing is there, he realizes he has spent years fearing a figment of his imagination. The past and the future are also imaginary constructs. They are thought forms which don't exist in this moment. We bring them into existence by thinking about them, which causes a corresponding emotion to match this thought, and if we believe this thought, then we spend our lives at the mercy of the emotions these thoughts cause.

HELL, HEAVEN, AGONY, DAMNATION, DEVIL, ANTI-CHRIST, PARADISE, etc. Why did they say such things? Because fear sells. They knew what people were afraid of at that time, and they knew how to use their fears against them. They still do the exact same thing today. They've just 'modernized' their lies; "SOW A SEED", "PAY YOUR TITHE", etc. There is no solid evidence whatsoever in what they tell you; life after death, hell, heaven etc. Unlike the moon and the stars, we know where they are but as for hell, we are yet to find its address and geographical coordinates, please if you do have it be kind enough to share to the world. Isn't it ironic how the preacher loves to tell the people that they should have faith and believe as written in a book of unknown authors? In my opinion, those claims are just as ridiculous as the claims that anyone that tries to illuminate people is an ANTI-CHRIST. They have ZERO evidence to back those claims up, but people still say them all the time. When I first read the bible, the constant threats stood-out as the biggest sign that something wasn't right.

"Most people would kill the truth if the truth would kill their religion"- Lemuel K. Washburn

One day on the streets of Alexandria, Egypt, in the year 415 or 416, a mob of Christian zealots led by Peter the Lector accosted a woman's carriage and dragged her from it into a church, where they stripped her and beat her to death with roofing tiles. They then tore her body apart and burned it. Who was this woman and what was her crime? Hypatia was the last great thinkers of ancient Alexandria and one of the first women to study and teach mathematics, astronomy and Philosophy. Though she is remembered for her gruesome death, she is one of the examples of the victimization of religion during the era of religious autocracy. She simply made the statement below:

"Fables should be taught as fables, myths as myths, and miracles as poetic fancies. To teach superstitions as truths is a most terrible thing. The child mind accepts and believes the, and only through great pain and perhaps tragedy can it be years later relieved of them. In fact, men will fight for a superstition quite as quickly as for a living truth- often more so, since a superstition is so intangible you cannot get at it to refute it,

but truth is a point of view, and so is changeable."

Abrahamic religions have spread over the centuries through fear, terror, slavery and wars. Hypatia's case is just one of the many cases of victimization of free-thinkers by religious institutions and people. And Hypatia was right with her statement above; she was killed because of superstition. Anyone who says religion brought peace, morality, education and civilization is either ignorant or willfully lying.

When I began questioning my faith and expressing some of the things I found very irrational in the bible and the Christian faith in general, a lot of folks usually came-up to me to threaten me with the wrath of God. When I began sharing biblical gaffes, and questioning the authencity of the bible through the social media, a lot of individuals on my friends list at that time were filled with great contempt and loathe for me. None of them could discredit my points and arguments, all they did was threaten me that God will deal will me harshly. You'll hear them say stuffs like "Imoh you are playing with fire", "You have sold your soul to the Devil", "repent now it is not late". Even some took it to another level with statements like "May God punish you", "let the fire of God come down and burn you", etc. You can see that these people had a wish to deal with me if it were possible; they wish there existed some power that could come down and exterminate my life. And to my suprise I was generously labelled an extremist by these guys.

I always find it confusing why people who belong to a religious practice whose Chief activity is to disturb the peace of others with loud public speakers, embarrass travelers and passersby with their creeds, deface the environment and streets with posters of their activities and above all, continually come on air to threaten others with their imaginary horror movies, will turn around and accuse another of extremism. I do not understand this at all.

The Abrahamic religion adherents are the only group of people in the history of the planet who score the highest points in the destruction of the planet than everyone else. Nobody does it like them. To crown it all, they consider themselves sane and others insane. This is where I am stuck between the cross roads of laughter and tears.

History has shown that that the Abrahamic religions spread through violence, war and slavery. And they have killed and destroyed people or group that disagreed with their fantasies. An example was Galileo Galilee who was arrested and later poisoned for asserting that the earth is not flat and that the sun does not circle the earth but the earth circles the sun. This is contrary to the words of the beliefs of the Church accorded to the scriptures.

"The further a society drifts from the truth, the more it'll hate those that speak it"- George Orwell

Contrary to the some arguments that these things happened in those days, it still happens today. An acquaintance, Gabriel Obinna whom I met in the journey of self-emancipation told me that he was rejected by his parents because he does not believe in the bible. In his words while narrating his story: "I became an atheist at the age of 19, now I'm 22 and my parents still believed I am a useless child! They refused to sponsor my college education because they felt I am wasted, I don't live with them anymore. I walk the street of Ibadan as an independent boy, working hard for possibilities. My supposed extended families in the village still call me a fool for not going to church. Most times I want to cry; most times I wish this world wasn't rapt with religion and that people live freely without any restriction on how they treat their fellow human beings. Every day I become stronger and confident. I have lived on my own, struggled on mine own and I still wake up with the assurance that I'll survive."

In the holy books, it is said that they (the believers) will suffer persecution, but that is not true, it is the religious people that persecute others including themselves. The unbeliever is the persecuted and victim of the religious.

An example of this victimization or should I say persecution was the case Of Mubarak Bala in the predominant Northern Muslim community of Nigeria:

Mubarak Bala, I've never met him, but an ex-Muslim he is, as I've learned from a mutual friend who speaks highly of him. Mubarak Bala was declared mentally unstable and then incarcerated in a psychiatric ward because he does not believe in Allah or any other fancy sky character which men insist must exist for other men to be deem morally and mentally fit. A victim of the evil-headed monster, religion he became. The story of Mubarak is quintessential of the madness of the totalitarian intimidation of religion in the modern world.

As at the time of his incarceration, all voices of plea for his freedom fell on deaf ears. The medical facility, his family and the state were conspiring to torture the apostate into submission to their creed. It is no longer news that Nigeria is toxically religious, thus the ruthlessness and corruption in corporation between the medical facility and his family which held him was bore out of the mass cultural sentiment of a typical religious individual that one who rejects the fallacy and tenets of their creed is an exhibit of the mentally unstable. In Nigeria, an atheist is first of all a mad man, and then an agent of Satan. As such, it was not too difficult for the parties involved: the medical facility, family to speak in unison and of course the state. The role of silence played by the state to intervene in the matter which met international condemnation only revealed where the sympathy of the state lies.

The secular community both local and the international weighed in, of which my pen couldn't refuse participation. My anger and irritation against the brother was natural since I've had similar encounter in the past. When I began debunking my childhood beliefs and defecating its final remains, I was tagged a psycho by acquaintances and strangers alike: "how can you say God does not exist? You are mad and need help!" They declared. Soon afterwards, when the cheap acrimonious diagnosis couldn't do any good, they graduated to "you are the anti-Christ", "you are possessed by demons", "you are an agent for Satan", etc. again after that one became over the hill, they coughed out a new one which I am currently dabbling with: "keep your beliefs to yourself and let us believe what we want to believe". Not too eager to declare my safety in the hands of my social doctors and arbiter of mental status, but unlike Mubarak Bala, I was excused with the indulgence of exercising my "madness".

Though in the same country, Mubarak unlike me was not lucky to be in the type of environment where he could be afforded the same freedom like mine. Unlike me, he is an apostate of Islam and we know that one is more likely to be killed by a devout Muslim for debunking Islam than knocked down by car on the Highway. It is easier for a Christian to deconvert than a Muslim. Muslims who wish to deconvert are faced with the threats of death and execution from their counterparts and as we assume, the fear of death surpasses the fear of all. Only one who has conquered fear can completely abdicate that which is not coherent with his reality irrespective of the consequence.

When Mubarak was victimized, nobody cared. When I mean nobody, I mean the civil rights group and human rights activists in the country. They were silent. Probably it was no abuse in their eyes, why? Because he is an atheist in a religious nation. The atheist is the one that unites the irritation of the different religious people against a single object. They should be grateful for this unity of irritation; they have agreed on one thing, at least.

We can't account for the number of deaths and destruction that has been brought on the human race through the spread of religion. The slave trade and colonization were brothers of religions and they brought so much turmoil and destruction wherever they set their feet on.

"They appealed to the worst obsessions of the human heart, sowing the seeds of discord and hatred in every land along the way. Brother denounced brother, wives informed against their husbands, mothers accused their children, dungeons were crowded with the innocent; the flesh of the good and true rotted in the clasp of chains; the flames devoured the heroic, and the name of the merciful God, his children were exterminated with famine, sword, and fire. Over the wild waves of battle rose and fell the banner of Jesus Christ. For sixteen hundred years the robes of the church were red with innocent blood. The ingenuity of Christians was exhausted in devising punishment severe enough to be inflicted upon other Christians who honestly and sincerely differed with them upon any point whatever" – Robert Green Ingersoll, 1874

MORALITY AND THE RELIGIOUS

It is a myth that religion teaches any special kind of morality. Doctrines aren't the same as morals

In general, it is noted that the countries with highest crime rate, unemployment, human rights abuse, illiteracy, corruption and under-development are the most religious. Nigeria is the best evidence in the entire universe that religion does nothing to people's morality. Nigeria being the most religious nation on earth is the best boast of morality gifted by religion. The behavioural repertoire of most religious Nigerians is cognitively evil. They are illustrious of a dragon, when allowed to open its mouth, vomits from its belly its true components. They have this mental projection of harm and destruction on another person. I remember sometime ago a lady on my Facebook page said to me "I curse you" simply because I narrated the gaffes in the bible. She was in a habit of constantly sending me threat messages, curses and prayers of destruction. She particularly told me that God told her that he'll kill me. And this is the attribute of love that religion produces in people? How saddening. She must have been thinking that she is doing a noble work for God. She is not alone in this. Her predecessors usually burned the likes of me on stakes.

The Christian doctrine is loud in its sermon of love. "Love thy neighbor as thyself", they repeat incessantly. Their acclaimed love is a theoretical myth and I do not blame them for this practical hypocrisy because expecting love from them is an unfair and impossible demand. How can they love their neighbours as themselves, when their God does not even love Satan as himself? Expecting religion to practice what they preach is like expecting a hyena to be a friendly animal just because it makes a noise that sounds like laughter. Religion makes people full of hate and vexation and they always hide under the cover of their so called religious morality to perpetrate their evil. Sometimes the best way of cohabiting with religious and provocative people is to simply understand they are idiots; register some condolence with them rather than a conflict.

Religion is the enterprise of men and their God is the invention of their alter-ego. This is the reason why men catch feelings for God and get offended on his behalf. When a person says you are insulting his beliefs or saying blasphemous things against God, he is simply telling you that you are hurting his feelings and ridiculing his alter-ego which he calls God.

A devastating act took place in a small town, Aluu in Rivers State, Nigeria where four young university students went to collect debt from a friend who was evading to pay-up, in the early hours of the morning. The debtor, unwilling to pay his debt and to teach his creditor a lesson, raised a false alarm in the neighborhood calling them armed robbers. There is nothing as senselessly terrifying like a mob of zealous religious people about to apprehend a perceived sinner and defaulter. If a religious man can singularly believe something ridiculous without evidence, then a mob of religious people is the worst thing that can befall an innocently accused person. The zealous mob accosted the young men and wasted no time in burning them alive after getting bored with lynching them with all manner of crude weapons. While the barbarism was freely exercised in the early hours of the morning, the large crowd of the community was comfortably recording this act on their mobile phones. On the video you would be irritated to discover that a crowd of enthusiast cheered as the barbaric men poured fuel on the young men and then set them ablaze. Even a farm animal is not killed in such a horrible way. Not even a single person in the crowd was moved to intervene; the spectating crowd was too concerned with recording this wickedness rather than calling the police. Just like that, innocent young men were conspired against and lynched to the spectatorship of a religious crowd in broad day light. Where is the morality? I ask. I thought people living in the most religious nation on earth are suppose to be the most moral and virtuous of men on earth. The community is a Christian community and 94% of residents in the state where this gruesome act took place are Christians. The men who set them ablaze were Christians and the spectators who watched with thrill are Christians. Watching such a horrible video will put a rational person in tears and pains as the four young men begged for their lives saying: "we are not thieves", "I beg you in the name of

God", but it fell on deaf ears. Even the religious man does not revere the name of his God. Religion does not make anyone moral, but rather, it robs the consciousness of man and nails his empathy on a casket.

Another incident equally took place when some people accused to be gays were accosted by Christians in Enugu city of Nigeria and they were burned alive. Yet again in the city of Warri, Nigeria, a girlie adult who was quietly walking on the street was confronted by a mob of homophobic blood thirsty religitards. After he was stripped naked by the mob who accused him of being "unnatural" because he developed a small size of pair of breasts and looked like a man, which according to them is unnatural and demonic. I am moved to say a man who denies God is a godly man and a man who professes God is a professional Devil. They have been many instances where people get lynched and burned to death by mobs for very miserly and superstitious reasons in this part of the world where religion is the mass cultural practice. In a city like Lagos, a mob of zealots have lynched a man to death over an accusation by a passerby that the suspect touched him with voodoo and then his genitals vanished. In the culture of believe without evidence of the religious, after lynching the accused to death will they now ask the accuser to show the crowd the evidence of his missing genitals. But it's too late, the did has already been done to an innocent poor man. Everything is to be feared about a mob of religious people. Senseless people in intimidating numbers are capable of any form of destruction.

Here is a short narration of one of the many bloody historic display of morality by the religious:

"The Christians, with their horses and swords and lances, began to slaughter and practice strange cruelty among them. They penetrated into the country and spared neither children nor the aged, nor pregnant

women, nor those in child labor, all of whom they ran through the body and lacerated, as though they were assaulting so many lambs herded in their sheepfold. They made bets as to who would slit a man in two, or cut off his head at one blow: or they opened up his bowels. They tore babes from their mothers' breast by the feet, and dashed their heads against the rocks. Others they seized by the shoulders and threw into the rivers, laughing and joking ... They spitted the bodies of other babes, together with their mothers and all who were before them, on their swords. They made a gallows just high enough for the feet to nearly touch the ground, and by thirteens, in honor and reverence of our Redeemer and the twelve Apostles, they put wood underneath and burned the Indians alive. They wrapped the bodies of others entirely in dry straw, binding them in it and setting fire to it; and so they burned them. They cut off the hands of all they wished to take alive. They generally killed the lords and nobles in the following way. They made wooden gridirons of stakes, bound them upon them, and made a slow fire beneath: thus the victims gave up the spirit by degrees, emitting cries of despair in their torture."~ Bartolomeo de las Casas (1484-1566) (Short Report on the Destruction of the Indies)

FEDERICK DOUGLASS who was an American slave in the 18th century had his own share of experience of the morality which the religious displays:

"I therefore hate the corrupt, slaveholding, women-whipping, cradle-plundering, partial and hypocritical Christianity of the land. Indeed, I can see no reason, but the most deceitful one, for calling the religion of this land Christianity. I look upon it as the climax of all misnomers, the boldest of all frauds, and the grossest of all libels. Never was there a clearer case of 'stealing the livery of the court of heaven to serve the devil in.' I am filled with unutterable loathing when I contemplate the religious pomp and show, together with the horrible inconsistencies, which every where surround me. We have men-stealers for ministers, women-whippers for missionaries, and cradle-plunderers for church members. The man who wields the blood-clotted cowskin during the week fills the pulpit on Sunday, and claims to be a minister of the meek and lowly Jesus. . . . The slave auctioneer's bell and the church-going bell chime in with each other, and the bitter cries of the heart-broken slave are drowned in the religious shouts of his pious master. Revivals of religion and revivals in the slave-trade go hand in hand together. The slave prison and the church stand near each other. The clanking of fetters and the rattling of chains in the prison, and the pious psalm and solemn prayer in the church, may be heard at the same time. The dealers in the bodies and souls of men erect their stand in the presence of the pulpit, and they mutually help each other. The dealer gives his blood-stained gold to support the pulpit, and the pulpit, in return, covers his infernal business with the garb of Christianity. Here we have religion and robbery the allies of each other—devils dressed in angels' robes, and hell presenting the semblance of paradise."

---A Narrative of the Life of Frederick Douglass, an American Slave (1818-1895).

One must have heard robust claims by religious apologists, especially from the adherents of Christianity and Islam that great empires and nations of the world today were founded by Christians and Muslims. And they were founded on Christian and Islamic principles as the case may be. This misconception is not only historically false but fraudulent in logic.

The truth be told, no great empire and nation on earth today was founded on any moral principles of Christianity or Islamic principles. Most of them have directly and indirectly been founded on the principles of the universal practice, inherent of mankind; Armed Robbery! And the moment they can no longer continue as Armed Robbers, they fall.

What is Armed Robbery? It is the use of force, arms and violence in extorting the properties (be it intellectual, material, art, craft, etc) of other people. In this process, the Armed Robber may deploy vices such as blackmail, coercion, duress, deception, and subversion. I cannot place any ancient empire, the Babylonian, the Persian, the Roman, etc that was not founded on the sword and on the blood of conquered nations. In the modern world, you think of the British Empire, founded on the blood of colonies, where through the force of arms, they stole lands and resources.

What of the American empire? A country founded by an exodus of armed bandits and gun wielding religious people, who wiped out entire colonies of red Indians and took their lands and resources by force. What of the war of independence from Britain? Was it not by force of arms that a colony cast off its own master? What of the slave trade, by which Western Nations first built their economies, was it not on the back of the blood of forcefully taken slaves, in the most immoral type of robbery ever known to man? Or is it what the Japanese did during their rise? Ask the Chinese their experience with Japanese Imperialism. Or is it the rise of modern China on the back of the communist revolution? Or of Russia, the era of Lenin and Stalin? Or of Modern Iraq and the wars of by the Ayatollahs, or of Ancient Israel, wherein the Old Testament is one continuous litany of forceful land grabs in the name of Yahweh! Or of modern Israel, and the seized lands of the

Palestinians. Or of the Salaudeen Wars, the Ottoman Empire, the wars of Uthman Dan Fodio, etc?

All great empires are founded on force, arms, and wars. They forcefully grabbed and subverted their victims. These are standard principles of the universal religion of Armed Robbery by mankind. But then, it suddenly occurs on me that I could be wrong and the people who claim that these empires were founded on religious principles may actually be right. It may be that I am actually the ignorant one and that, as they have said, taking up arms and seizing lands and resources by force are actually Christian and Islamic principles on which these nations were founded. In which case, I should apologize. Perhaps, even the Christians and Muslims operate the same principles as the universal practice of Armed Robbery. Who knows?

"Men never commit evil so fully and joyfully as when they do it for religious convictions"- Blaise Pascal

---

I saw a short video of a girl child acclaimed to be 4 years of age who was stripped naked in a church congregation and tagged a devil and tormented child. Why? According to the video which was spoken in French and the interpreter translated to English for the congregation (which should ordinarily be presumed that the incident took place in Francophone speaking African nation), the child is accused of demon possession and satanic influence because she developed breasts and was pregnant, which is obviously from an abuser. But the preacher and the congregation did not see that, what they saw was a demon possessed child being pregnant at age 4. However, the age of this child cannot be confirmed and the true place where such an abuse took place is not stated on the short video. However, it is possible for a child to develop breasts before age 7 or 8. The child is merely through what is called "Precocious

Puberty". It is often advised that parents who notice such should report to a pediatrician for examination in case there is an underlying health problem to be treated in the child. But ignorance gifted by religion refuses to know these things; the parents of this young child rather took the child to a pastor for theocratic diagnosis and treatment. The grave offenses here baffled me.

There are two grave offences committed here.

1. The child was abused by being stripped naked in front of the whole congregation of the church, while the sheeple (including her wards) cheered to this.

2. By asserting that her pregnancy and the resulting breast being grown is the work of the devil, the evil perpetrator of this heinous crime of child abuse, I mean the guy who molested this innocent child, is being protected against justice. This is unkind and gruesome, to say the least.

The image and psyche of that innocent child is battered. This is an example of one of the countless cases of the disastrous religious morality. Yes, man is evil, we know. There are certainly some atheists, agnostics, freethinkers or humanists who are not good in any form. That's incontrovertible too. But there has never been any way these set of people claim any deity told or inspired them to do whatever they do. They are simply responsible for their actions.

However, if you want to see foolishness in full display and the display of mass coldness and lack of judgment, visit a religious centre and community. If you want to comfortably commit evil, use religion.

During the week of Ramadan, a mob of devout Muslims roasted four members of an Ahmadi family alive (including 2 children) over a "blasphemous facebook post." The Ahmadiyya also known as the Ahmadi Muslims is a

Muslim sect regarded by both the Shiites and Sunnis as heretical because they believe that God sent Mirza Ghulam Ahmad (1835-1908) an acclaimed Muhajadid (divine reformer), Mahdi (Guided One) and the promised Messiah awaited by the Muslims and above all, the Ahmadi Muslims are peaceful and not violent. Houses were looted after the mob gathered outside the properties on the pretext they were protesting over an alleged defacing of a picture of the Kaabah on Facebook by an Ahmadi Muslim.

The allegation of blasphemy was vehemently denied by local Ahmadis. Ahmadis regard the Kaabah in Makkah as Islam's Holiest Sacred Mosque. This took place in Pakistan. The slaughtering of Ahmadi Muslims is commonplace in Pakistan, where hate-filled sermons from extremist religious clerics goad worshipers to attack minorities. The Ahmadis are specifically targeted because of their belief in their founder as the promised Messiah, a belief that extremist clerics say makes Ahmadis liable to be killed. And is this the morality I hear they say that religion gives to people?

I am yet to meet a religious man whose behavior and mentality is good enough to be worthy of my ardent emulation. A religious man is a hypocrite in denial; a self-styled moralist and adjudicator of others. They have this hoity-toity mentality that they're better than others who don't belong to their religion or sect. Even among the religious, they do not even like themselves. You'll hear something like this: "Thank God I'm not a Catholic, I am not worshipping the devil like them", says the non-catholic Christians. The Jehovah witnesses will think their doctrine is far better and correct than the others, the Catholic think same, the Pentecostals think they are all blind people, meanwhile the Sabbath day Christians are laughing at all of them. All of them have this trait and mentality of "I-am-following-the-right-beliefs", "The-others-are-blind", etc.

They have these traits of selfishness in them. When Christian A is doing better, he'll say God is blessing him better than Christian B. On other hand, Christian B who is doing so badly will say "God is testing my faith" or "God knows what is best for me". If by chance Christian B starts doing better than Christian A, Christian B will assert "My God has finally visited me, he has lifted my head above my neighbours. Those who looked down on me, now look up to me". And of course the preachers are always there to masturbate their selfish desires and egos with sermons to trigger their self-importance.

Religion is a virus. The religious man is a social nuisance and social terrorist. If religion made people good, we wouldn't be here complaining about it, they would have been no need writing this book in the first place. If religion made people any better, the world would have been safer, tolerant, loving and peaceable. If religion made people better, the most religious of nations like Pakistan, Afghanistan, Ghana, Zimbabwe, etc would have been the least corrupt of nation on earth, but that is not the case. It is funny how countries like Japan, South Korea, France, and Singapore who are less religious are not as corrupt as their religious counterparts. Where do they get their morality from? Is it just a coincidence that nations which the religious nations regard as immoral and hopeless infidels happen to be performing very poorly in feats like corruption, poverty, violence and under-development? Does it not appear to them that good fortune seems to be found more in the homes of those whom God or Allah despises in his holy books but conspires against them who hold tenaciously to his creeds? Too good to be true, isn't it?

I see religion as an ass; anyone can beat it as he/she desires. Like Karl Marx said, "Religion is the opium of the people" he went ahead to enumerate that religion is the enemy and must be eliminated for man to be totally free. Religion has done considerably well in fracturing the morals of men than catering for their virtue it professes. Religious people are either hypocrite, intransigent or fanatical in social and political, philosophical, and even scientific ideologies; one needs not search very far, for its fruits are palpable for all to see.

Religion has really drawn some folks into the deception that they can adjudicate others and assuage themselves as upright and morally fettle. Hypocrisy everywhere! In my personal observation, I have come to a pseudo-conclusion that it is people with self-acclaimed morality i.e. the religious folks that commit the most hideous of depravity. The self-styled moralists and adjudicators of actions, dress codes, languages and opinions of others are the real problems of the society. Such individuals tend to be lack-luster in ideas and ideals; no creativity, no inspiration. And that is a core problem of the African society and third world nations in general, because these types of people tend to dominate their clime in numbers and in all spheres of the society, and yet you will find corruption and human rights abuse is very endemic in these religious third world countries, and this makes me wonder: "of what use is their so-called religious morality?" When one does not have imaginary friends and imaginary places he wishes to go, he'll value the real life and implore his natural endowment usefully in order to obtain the best of sanity and prosperity he can ever wish for. If these types of people are in a particular geographical unit en mass, then that place will definitely express the concept of humanity.

"Muslims are the first victims of Islam. Many times I have observed in my travels in the Orient that fanaticism comes from a small number of dangerous men who maintain the others in the practice of religion by terror. To liberate the Muslim from his religion is the best service that one can render him. — E. Renan

ISLAM AND VIOLENCE

Many often one may get inundated with the arguments that the religion of Islam is peaceful by the Muslim apologists who strive so hard to assuage the monstrosity by their fellow Koran adherents. The truth is: the avowed peacefulness of Islam is self-evident in its practice by its adherents. One of the excuses they make is that Mohammed was a peaceful man who taught his followers same and that Muslims lived peacefully for centuries, fighting only in self-defense and necessity. "True Muslims will never act aggressively", the moderate and liberal Muslims will argue.

Quran (4:95) puts it this way:

"Not equal are those believers who sit (at home) and receive no hurt, those who strive and fight in the cause of Allah with their goods and persons. Allah had granted a grade higher to those who strive and fight with their goods and persons than those who sit (at home). Unto all (in faith) hath Allah promised good: but those who strive and fight hath he distinguished above those who sit (at home) by a special reward."

The above passage from the Koran is very clear on the status of the peaceful and radical Muslims. It criticizes the peaceful Muslim and the reward of such a Muslim is not equal with those who strive hard and fight against non believers. The violent ones are the ones in whom Allah is pleased while the peaceful Muslim is one who is of a lesser value in their eyes of Allah and will be punished with hell.

Quran 9:38-39 announces:

"O ye who believe! What is the matter with you, that, when ye are asked to go forth in the cause of Allah, ye cling heavily to the earth? Do ye prefer the life of this world to the hereafter? But little is the comfort of this life, as compared with the hereafter. Unless ye go forth, He will punish you with a grievous penalty and put others in your place."

"Islam is a religion of peace"; this is a great lie and a ridiculous parody that is analogous to the statement that "a lion is a domestic animal" and "fire is not a dangerous element". Another myth is the statement that jihad is a "spiritual struggle" and not a "holy war", as some Islam apologists may argue. Others argue that the concept of jihad is defensive rather than offensive. Jihadists and terrorists who take up arms are doing exactly as dictated by the Koran and exemplified by Mohammed.

"If Christ were here there is one thing he would not be... a Christian." --- Mark Twain. On that note may I add, if Mohammed were here, there is one thing he would certainly be; a Muslim. But I understand you people call them terrorists and Islamic fundamentalists. Well, there is no such thing as a terrorist or an Islamic fundamentalist, we just have a practicing Muslim, or a Muslim at faith.

Mohammed organized 65 military campaigns in the last ten years of his life and he personally led 27 of them. The more powerful he became, the smaller the excuses he needed to go to battle until he finally began attacking tribes merely because they were not yet part of his growing empire. Even if Mohammed were to be alive in this age, the so called moderate Muslims will still accuse him of not practicing Islam and will still go ahead to say he is not a Muslim. If you do not know the content of your holy books don't deny those who are practicing it differently from your comprehension; it is self-denial. ISIS, Boko Haram, Al Qaeda, Al Shabab, Hamas and others did not wake-up one morning to unleash terror from reading mills and boon or sermons from a stand-up comedian.

After the death of Mohammed, his successor Abu Bakr followed suite, declaring allied tribes which wanted to go their way "apostates", and slaughtering anyone who refuses to remain a Muslim and he was very successful with his blood and violent campaigns. There is no such thing as tolerance in Islam

Quran 8:39 asserts:

"And fight them until there is no more fitnah (unbelief) and religion should be only for Allah"

The historical context of this text is of the submission that the Meccans refused Mohammed access to their city after hajj. He had prior declared war on Mecca and consequently was evicted. It was Mohammad's desire to destroy the polytheistic idol worship of the Meccans. The excuse for declaring war on unbelievers is merely on the grounds of their unbelief. Like the typical arrogance in the concept of monotheism, every other belief or unbelief is not to be condoned.

Ibn Ishaq/Hisham 324 says that Muhammad stated that **"Allah MUST have no rivals"**. Even in the absence of other religious beliefs, Muslims turn on each other. It is not a coincidence that countries like Iraq, Iran, Afghanistan, Pakistan, etc where are there are little or no other religions other Islam, suffer incidences of terrorism and bomb blasts of Shiites against the Sunnis and vice versa. Islam is a preying ideology; it must always seek for whom or a cause to fight against.

A Muslim scholar shared this in a large online Muslim group:

A Muslim has 2 'Eidan (Eids) and Fridays only.

A Muslim does not believe in nationalism.

A Muslim does not stand for anyone but Allah.

A Muslim is not allowed to observe moments of silence.

A Muslim is not allowed to place floral wreaths at graves.

A Muslim does not take his shoes off out of reverence to people; dead or alive neither does he stand up as a form of respect to anybody.

A Muslim is neither allowed to innovate in the deen or take from the Kuffar (Kuffar or Kaffirs is the plural of the word Kaffir which means unbeliever or infidel in Arabic/Islam)

The celebration of Victory Day, Independence Day, Wedding Anniversary, Memorial Service, Birthdays, New Year are all haram (unlawful). Ditch it. Trash it!

The devout Muslim has a dynamite emotions and temperamental view of life. They are volatile in their intolerance to all things. Almost everything offends them in the modern and civilized world. The devout Muslim is offended by: homosexuality, Christianity, Buddhism, atheism, Confucianism, other Muslims, women rights, feminism, civilization, Judaism, fashion, music, art, media, dance, beauty pageant, pornography, education, western education, rule of law, free speech, paganism, evolution theory, science/facts, poetry, tattoo, tolerance, etc just to name a few.

With or without the Islamists and fundamentalists, an average devout Muslim is a potential anarchy and passive intolerant despot. Muslims kill people who drew the cartoons of Prophet Mohammed. They should kill people who are named after him, they are the bigger cartoons.

Before the existence of Boko Haram in Northern Nigeria, Christians and non-Muslims were living in gamble security. The devout Muslim is naturally configured by his doctrine to be paranoid, intolerant and volatile at anything that threatens his spurious religious sentiments. There is no such thing as a comedy or sense of humor around the doctrine of devout Muslims.

In 1953 the first known riot in the majority Muslim Northern Nigeria ended in a bloody manner which led to the death of over 25 non-Muslims and southerners. In 1966, a similar bloody riot took place because of a radio report that Muslims are segregated in Southern Nigeria. In the 1980s, a serious civil outbreak took place in Kafanchan, a town in the Northern Nigeria and in 2010, rampaging Muslims went loose slaughtering an estimate of 500 people. All these and many more countless bloody conflicts were instigated by civil Muslims with no elements of insurgency. Just a mere revolution and irritation against the non-Muslims for very miserly reasons (miserly for the rational person though).

An example of such miserly reason was when a High school teacher took the Koran from a student who was concentrating in the Koran while the non-Muslim teacher was teaching in class. Boom! All hell was let loose in Northern Nigeria because of this.

The average devout Muslim wants to be respected, feared and of course to have a totalitarian control over the non-believer and to eliminate every form of unbelief but on the other hand, they will not return the favor. The devout

Muslim finds no difficulty in striking, burning and slaughtering an erring non-Muslim especially when it's got everything to do with an accusation of blasphemy of Islam. All a devout Muslim needs is a little or no excuse to go on rampage against their unsuspecting non-believing neighbours. The Danish Mohammed cartoon incident which took place in a far away Europe was all they needed to unleash mayhem in Northern Nigeria and other climes where they are found. When Nigeria wanted to host the Miss World beauty pageant, a newspaper columnist in the spirit of euphoria of the ink remarked that the contestants are so beautiful that even Mohammed would not have mind taking a bride amongst them. It was during the month of Islamic activities. All hell was let loose, the devout Muslims went paranoid, destroying buildings in Northern Nigeria and killing non believers in their clime. These acts of destruction are often carried out by the ordinary Muslim adherent with non-militant mindset, just a mere civil muslim's revolt against the non-believers. Any mass Muslim protest against actions considered anti-Islam is often bloody; neither life nor property is safe. As a matter of fact, destruction is certain.

Whenever there is a report of an anti-Islamic remark or action in anywhere in the world, devout Muslims all over the world usually come out in their numbers to protest. Whether the act took place in America or Europe, one will find Muslims in Nigeria, Lebanon, Iran, Yemen, Saudi Arabia, Pakistan Afghanistan, India, Iraq and the rest of the world coming out in numbers to vent their anger, burning American and British flags, carrying volatile placards with war-like remarks. During this period, America and European governments will issue security alerts both at home and abroad, cautioning their citizens to take to safety. Non Muslim embassies in these Muslim nations at the time are not safe; they shut down and their citizens are flown out by their government over safety concerns. But when there is mass protest in European and non-Muslim countries like the Britain and the US, the embassies of Muslim nations are not worried about their safety and they go about doing their normal businesses. On a contrast, when non-Muslims are abused and killed by the fundamentalists in Iraq, Lebanon, Syria and elsewhere, these same devout Muslims, see nothing and hear nothing. They do not come out to protest. Never will one hear that Muslims issued a Fatwa against insurgent groups like ISIS, Boko Haram, Hamas, Al Qaeda, etc. The loud silence of the moderate Muslim is implicating. They are either passively sympathizing with these terror Jihadist groups who are spilling blood to spread Islam or they are just cowards whose voices are only loud where they can easily oppress the non-Muslims or join their mass society in venting their anger and irritation against the West and non-Muslims. Either ways, they are guilty. They cannot be claiming that fundamentalism is not part of Islam and yet look away and do nothing when the fundamentalist Muslim perpetuates crimes against humanity in the name of Jihad and Islam.

There is nothing more foolish and dangerous like living in the mist of devout Muslims. In times of great scandal against their faith, you'll secure a costly lesson about their peacefulness. A Muslim is most likely to be peaceful when:

- Brought up in a rich background and educated (however not a guarantee)

- Had a transition of most and all his teenage/youthful life amongst non-believers

- Lived, worked and had relationships with non-Muslims for the most part of his life.

- Residing and working in a largely controlled area by non-faiths

Muslims with the above credentials are often regarded by the more volatile ones as hypocrites, ignorant, unbelieving Muslims, etc. The Ahmadiyyas who are the liberal Islamic sets, these Muslims are peaceful to the core, however at a daily bloody cost. The Sunnis, Shiites and the rest of the crew hunt them to death everywhere. They regard their kind of Islam as blasphemous. If the Ahmadis are not spared and accorded some protection by their colleagues, how much more a 100% Kaffir (unbeliever)?

The bloodiness, intolerance and totalitarianism of Islam did not begin today, it was earlier revealed by the most faithful followers and family members of Mohammad who turned on each other. There were four caliphs in the first 25 years after Mohammed's death, and each of which was his trusted companion. Three of these four were murdered by those allied with the son of the first caliph. The fourth caliph was murdered in the midst of a bloody conflict with the fifth caliph who began a 100 year dynasty of debauchery which was soon ended by widespread bloodbath of the descendants of Muhammad's uncle (who wasn't even a Muslim).

Muhammad's own daughter, Fatima and her husband Ali survived the years of paganism in Mecca but they could not survive the years of the proliferation of Islam after Mohammad's demise. Fatima died of stress of persecution within 3 months and Mohammed's son-in-law Ali was later assassinated by Muslim rivals. Their son (Mohammed's grandson) was killed in battle by a faction that became today's' Sunnis while his people became the Shiites. Other relatives and personal friends of Muhammad were caught-up and entangled in the mist of the bloody conquest between the rival groups, and which metamorphosed into sub-divisions as Islam expanded through the ages.

Muslim apologists always argue that true Muslims do not take the lives of a human being let alone another Muslim.

But it is surprising how they give blind eyes to the bloody conquests and spread of Islam through its 1,400 years of existence. Mohammed who held his favourite wife and daughter; Aisha and Fatima respectively as the perfect model of the Muslim woman only led to the war between the followers of Fatima and Aisha in the violent civil wars that followed his death.

The definition of a "true Muslim" is made clear in Quran 9:88 and many other verses in the Quran – the true believer **"strives and fights with their wealth"**.

9: 123 clearly admonishes:

"Those who believe! Fight those of the unbelievers who are near to you and let them find in you hardness". The hypocritical Muslim is described in the Koran as one who sits at home refusing to join the clarion call of jihad. There is no tolerance in Islam.

The Koran contains at least 109 verses that exhort Muslims to wage war against non believers. Muhammad clearly left his followers and men with the command to wage war against the Jews, Christians, Persians, polytheists (who eventually are the Hindus). Muslim armies through the centuries invaded unsuspecting neighbors and lands, plundering them of loot, their women, taking them as slaves and forcing them to pay tax or risk being fed to their swords. This terrorism did not begin today, it is inherently part of Islam in its ideology to wage war, enslave, kill, plunder and mostly destroy other beliefs. It is no coincidence that the terrorists and jihadists all over the world hold sway to Islam and the teaching of Mohammed.

The Arab slave trade was open for 1300 years until the pressure and force from western powers drove the Arab nations to declare the practice of slavery as illegal. However, this declaration is only in theory. Unlike the Germans who apologized to the world over the totalitarianism and evil of the Nazi government of Hitler, the Arab world has never apologized over the victimization and bloody conquests of jihad and slavery.

No other religion on earth has consistently produce terrorists in the name of God like Islam. The most dangerous Muslims are the radicals and conservatives who adhere to the strict conformity of the teachings of the Koran literally, to spread Islam and the shariah law, willy-nilly. They are the ones we call the fundamentalists, who in the absence of "infidels" will turn on their fellow Muslims especially the moderate and liberal Muslims. The peaceful Muslim apologist only holds sway to a handful of verses which speaks of tolerance. However this same moderate or liberals are referred to as hypocrites for not participating in the brutality against non believers like their radical peers. The bloodiness of the Quran out numbers its serenity and the fruits of its ideology is made manifest by the purists. Those who are considered as moderates or liberal Muslim are merely people who give blind eyes to the perversion of the bloody conquest in the religion or are merely ignorant of the texts and teachings in the Quran. The so called religion of peace is by no means peaceful; the behavior of those who practice Islam, its history and the contents of its holy book speaks clearly for the so called religion of peace.

Some moderate Muslim apologists believe that Islam would never support killing innocent people and Allah in the Holy Koran never advocated killings. They will in fact disclaim Islamic terrorists as a few misguided individuals and that true Islam is against violence.

But how true is this? The Muslims who perpetrate crimes in the name of Islam and Allah disagree with them and in fact labels them false Muslims. One may wonder the following about the Muslim fundamentalist:

- Are they completely misguided?

- Where did they get this distorted ideology?
- How did they come to believe that killing innocent people pleases God?
- Does Islam really preach violence?
- Does it command the Muslims to kill the non-believers?
- These extremists are they actually doing what their holy book says and practicing as their prophet practiced?

The Koran will provide us with the answers since it is called the words of Allah. First all, it is important for the non Arabic Muslim to read the Koran in his or her understandable language and then apply critical thinking. The Koran clearly highlights the following:

- That the Muslim should not make friends with the Jews and Christians- (Quran 5:51)
- Prohibits the Muslim from befriending a non-believer even if that non-believer is his father or brother (Quran 9:23), (Quran 3:28)
- Fight the unbelievers until they pay the Jizya (a penalty tax for non-Muslims living under Islamic rules) with willing submission and feel themselves subdued -(Quran 9:29)
- Murder the unbelievers and treat them harshly- (Quran 9:123)
- Orders the Muslim to fight unbelievers until no other religion except Islam is left (Quran 2:193)

Dr. Ali Sina, an Iranian Muslim Apostate and Islam critic was asked:

"Is Islam as bad as depicted in your website? How come most of my Muslims friends are moderate and nice people?" Here is the answer by Dr. Ali Sina:

My simple answer is yes Islam is as bad as we depict it to be. Please do not mistake "Islam" with "Muslims". Muslim people are mostly good people. They are our families, friends and kin folks. Now, if any of them wants to practice true Islam, then they will become terrorists in today's standards. You see, Islam is a belief-system. It is an ideology that calls for Islam to reign supreme. Our site is against Islam, not against Muslims. We are against hate and against using violence against anyone, and that includes Muslims.

Now, Islam as a belief-system is a supremacist ideology. If you say that to a Muslim person, they will deny it mostly because they do not know their holy text. This is like any other religion. Take most Christians that tell you they are Christians, you will find out quickly that most of them do not know their Bible that much. The same applies to Muslims, most of them do not know much about the Qur'an, Hadith or Sirat. So, when you tell them Islam is a supremacist religion, they'll deny that. If you use their holy text to show them that, they'll say you are taking things "out of context".

Now, I just claimed that Islam is a bigoted supremacist religion, without using any evidence. Let me just give you some of the evidence. I invite anyone to study Islam's holy book, the Qur'an, and its supplements (books of Hadith and Sirat) and you will find much more evidence. Here is partial evidence:

a. In a free society, one is free to change his religion. In Islam, a Muslim who leaves Islam (becomes an atheist, agnostic, believer in another religion) is punished by death. This is the punishment for apostasy. You see, Islam considers itself the only true religion. All other beliefs are at fault. Islam aims at asserting its "truth" by force, threats, and killing of "renegades". Other religions may believe their way is the only right way, but you do not see them going after those who leave the faith with the sole purpose of killing them. Can you see how supremacist Islam is?

b. In a free society, all individuals are treated equally with regard to their taxation system. Not so in Islam. There is a tax system for Muslims and another for Non-Muslims. There is a special protection tax for non-Muslims called "Jizya". Non-Muslims pay it just to be able to live there. Non-Muslims are not allowed, in an Islam-proper society to run for office, or have any important positions in the government or Military. Such positions are available only for Muslims. Can you see how supremacist and evil Islam is?

c. Islam assumes rights for itself not available for others. Let us say, you want to marry a Muslim girl. As a man, you have to convert to Islam; otherwise, you won't be allowed to marry her. On the other side, if a Muslim man wants to marry a non-Muslim girl, he can, and the kids are Muslims by law.

d. Islam is also a misogynistic religion. In Qur'an 4:34 a man can beat his wife in certain situations. The woman cannot do the same to the man. A man can marry up to 4 women (plus he can have more as a right-hand procession). A woman can't do the same. A woman inherits half of what her brother gets.

Among Muslims there is no consensus. So Sunnis kill the Shiites, the Shiites kill the Sunnis and everyone kills the Ahmadis. When the Wahhabi and Salafi comes along, they kill everybody.

The fact is that since the beginnings of Islam, even during the time of Muhammad Muslims have been killing Muslims because one group did not accept the faith of other group.

Muhammad ordered some Muslims be burned in their mosque because someone said they have gone astray. Ali massacred four thousand unarmed Khawarijites who had sat in the mosque in protest in one day. So if you allow yourself to kill those who do not believe in your so called truth, you have given license to yourself to kill anyone you want. That is all the excuse you need to terminate anyone you dislike. Of course your version of truth is different from mine, so should I kill you or should you kill me?

People generally convert to Islam only "in terror or in quest of power, or to avoid heavy taxation, or to escape humiliation, or if taken prisoner, or because of infatuation with a Muslim woman."- Ibn Kammuna , as quoted in the works of Ibn Warraq "WHY I AM NOT A MUSLIM"

JIHADISM

"Islam is the religion of peace", the Muslim apologist tries so hard to explain. No other religion on earth struggles so hard to assert itself as peaceful with an embarrassing effort like Islam. It is a mere exercise of rhetoric in futility. If Islam was a religion of peace, the Muslim apologist won't struggle so hard to make his case and there would have been no need for such repetition of verbiage. Buddhists don't run around saying "Buddhism is a religion of peace", the same goes to Hinduism, Taoism and the rest of them. It is only Islam that suffers with the guilt and burden to assuage itself of the war and terrorism that is carried-out in its name. But the more they say Islam is a religion of peace, the more the insurgents in Pakistan, Afghanistan, Iraq, Lebanon, Mali, Central African Republic, Kenya, Northern Nigeria, etc, keeps making a mess of their joke.

Jihadism is a long practiced Islamic ideology which Mohammed used as a tool to kill his opponents and spread Islam. Mohammed was not a diplomatic man. His many war games, slave trades and raiding speak for itself. And he exhorted his followers to exterminate non-Muslims in their mist and spread the poisonous ideology through sweat and blood. The numerous verses in the Quran and the Hadith speaks for itself, which I've shared and will share more. Islamic scholars and philosophers spoke greatly of the importance of Jihadism to the Muslim. Some Muslim apologists who claim that Jihad is a spiritual warfare or a war fought on self-dense are actually being dishonest or ignorant of the doctrine of jihadism in Islam.

We can find hundreds of books written by well-known Islamic authorities (Islamic Chintabid or thinker) on Jihad. A few examples of historical events and comments should be enough to show the foundation that Jihad in Islamic history was primarily a war against the infidels. Here are some examples:

In his book, "Jurisprudence in Muhammad's Biography" the Azhar scholar, Dr. Muhammad Sa'id al-Buti wrote the following: **"The Holy War (Islamic Jihad), as it is known in Islamic Jurisprudence, is basically an offensive war. This is the duty of Muslims in every age when the needed military power becomes available to them. This is the phase in which the meaning of Holy war has taken its final form. Thus the apostle of God said: 'I was commanded to fight the people until they believe in Allah and his messages….. (Page 134, 7th edition) ".**

Dr. Buti went further adding in the same book (page-263): **The apostle of Allah started to send military detachments from among his followers to the various Arab tribes which were scattered in the Arab Peninsula to carry out the task of calling (these tribes) to accept Islam. If they did not respond, they (Muslims) would** kill them. That was during the 7th Hegira year. The number of the detachments amounted to ten."

In another page of the same work of Al-Buti quoted: **"The concept of Holy War (Jihad) in Islam does not take into consideration whether defensive or an offensive war. Its goal is the exaltation of the Word of Allah and the construction of Islamic society and the establishment of Allah's Kingdom on Earth regardless of the means. The means would be offensive warfare. In this case, it is the apex, the noblest Holy War. It is legal to carry on a Holy War."**

al-Baydawi, quoted in his book (The lights of Revelation, page-252): **"Fight Jews and Christians because they violated the origin of their faith and they do not believe in the religion of the truth (Islam), which abrogated all other religions. Fight them until they pay the poll-tax (Jizya tax) with submission and humiliation."**

Ibn Hisham Al Sohaily quoted Mohammed's famous line in his book (Al- Rawd al- Anaf, page-50, 51): **"No two religions are to exist in the Arab Peninsula."** Thus, Saudi Government does not allow any other religion in their country. In Saudi Arabia, atheism is punishable by death. This must be very tolerant and peaceful on the part of Islam.

A well-known Egyptian scholar, Sayyid Qutb, (Sayyid Qutb, Milestones, Revised Edition, chapter. 4, "Jihaad in the Cause of God") notes four stages in the development of jihad:

1. While the earliest Muslims remained in Mecca before fleeing to Medina, God did not allow them to fight;

2. Permission is given to Muslims to fight against their oppressors;

3. God commands Muslims to fight those fighting them;

4. God commands the Muslims to fight against all polytheists.

Sayyid Qutb views each stage to be replaced by the next stage in this order, the fourth stage to remain permanent). To justify the universal and permanent dimensions of jihad he cites the following Qur'anic passages:

Quran: 4:74-32: **They ought to fight in the way of God who have sold the life of this world for the life of the Hereafter; and whoever fights in the way of God and is killed or becomes victorious, to him shall We (God) give a great reward...**

Quran: 8:38-40: and **fight them until there is no oppression and the religion is wholly for God....**

Quran: 9:29-32: **Fight against those among the People of the Book (Jews and Christians) who do not believe in God and the Last Day, who do not forbid what God and His messenger have forbidden, until they are subdued and pay jizyah (tax on non-Muslims) ...**

Sayyid Qutb, however, pours scorn upon those who view jihad as solely defensive:

"... They are ignorant of the nature of Islam and of its function, and that it has a right to take the initiative for human freedom. Thus wherever an Islamic community exists which is a concrete example of the Divinely-ordained system of life, it has a God-given right to step forward and take control of the political authority so that it may establish the Divine system on earth, while it leaves the matter of belief to individual conscience."

Likewise, the popular Pakistani Muslim revivalist Abu'l Ala Mawdudi rejects any distinction between offensive and defensive jihad. So also, the distinguished contemporary Pakistani scholar, Fazlur Rahman, while recognizing the extensive presence of jihad in the Qur'an, rejects the stand of those modern Muslim apologists who have tried to explain the jihad of the early (Muslim) Community in purely defensive terms **(Fazlur Rahman, Islam (Chicago: University of Chicago Press, 1979) 37).**

According to the Encyclopedia of Islam, **"the fight is obligatory even when the unbelievers have not started it (E. Tyan, "Djihad", Encyclopaedia of Islam, 2nd ed. (Leiden: Brill, 1965).** In the words of Rudolph Peters: **the "ultimate aim of jihad is 'the subjection of the unbelievers' and 'the extirpation of unbelief'" (Rudolph Peters, "Jihad"- The Encyclopedia of Religion (New York: Macmillan, 1987) Vol. 8:88-91).**

In Jihad there is no limitation of force and any kind of practice (including sodomy) is permissible in so far it is for the spread of Islam and the extermination of non-believers. Following are excerpts from an address by London-based Shiite cleric Abdallah Al-Khilaf,

[TRANSCRIPT] Abdallah Al-Khilaf: First, we'd like to show you a fatwa, which appeared on the Lions of Sunna Internet forum. One Wahhabi Muslim wrote: "Dear Sheik, may Allah grant you martyrdom and black-eyed virgins in Paradise, I wanted to commit a martyrdom operation. I turned to Sheik Abu Dimaa Al-Qassab, who told me that they had invented a new and unprecedented form of martyrdom operations – explosive capsules are inserted into your anus.

"In order to train for this method of Jihad, you must consent to being sodomized for a period of time, so that your anus becomes wider, making room for the explosives. My question is whether I am permitted to allow one of the mujahedeen access to my anus, if my intentions are honorable, and the purpose is to train for Jihad by widening my anus?"

The sheik praised Allah and said: "**In principle, sodomy is forbidden. However, Jihad is more important. It is the pinnacle of Islam. If sodomy is the only way to reach this pinnacle of Islam, then there is no harm in it. The rule is that necessity makes the forbidden permissible. Something that is required in order to perform a duty becomes a duty in and of itself. No duty takes precedence over Jihad. Therefore, you must be sodomized... After you have been sodomized, you must ask Allah for forgiveness.**"

All of these authorities simply echo Islam's fundamental assumption that world sovereignty must be in the hands of Muslims.

Quran: 16:101: And when We put a revelation in place of (another) revelation, – and Allah knoweth best what He revealeth – they say: Lo! Thou art but inventing. Most of them know not.

On the basis of the above verse arose within the Muslim community the principle of Qur'anic interpretation, called naskh (abrogation) which stipulated that earlier peaceful verses could be abrogated by later militant verses, i.e., in the case of jihad the Meccan verses were abrogated by the Medinan verses. It is well known that many Muslim scholars in the early history of Islam contended that Qur'an 9:5, sometimes called "the verse of the sword", abrogated a host of peaceful passages in earlier portions of the Qur'an.

What it has signified in the past and signifies at present for masses of Muslims is well summarized in a statement by Ibn Khaldun (A.D. 1332-1406), Islam's great historian, sociologist and philosopher:

"**In the Muslim community, the holy war is a religious duty, because of the universalism of the (Muslim) mission and (the obligation to) convert everybody to Islam either by persuasion or by force. Therefore,** caliphate and royal authority are united in (Islam), so that the person in charge can devote the available strength to both of them at the same" *(Ibn Khaldun, The Muqaddimah, trans. by Franz Rosenthal (New York: Pantheon Books Inc., 1958) Vol. 1:473).*

The Translation of the Meanings of Sahih al-Bukhari, Vol. 1: xxiv-xliii:

So, it is incumbent upon us (Muslims) to follow the path which Allah's Messenger (Muhammad) adopted to avoid polytheism and heresy in all its shapes and to take the Holy Qur'an and the Prophet's Traditions as torches in front of us to guide us. We have to teach our brethren and convey the Message to non-Muslims all over the world as much as possible in order to save them from the Hell-fire. We have to prepare ourselves to stand in the face of our enemy and to possess the means of power and to participate in the progress of useful industries in order to protect our religion and be powerful enough to face our enemy, as Allah, the Elevated says in Surat al-Anfal (8:60):

Qur'an: 8:60: **Against them (kaffirs) make ready your strength to the utmost of your power, including steeds of war (tanks, places, missiles and other weapons, etc.) to strike terror into the (hearts of) the Enemy of Allah and your enemy, and others beside, whom you may not know, but whom Allah does know. Whatever you shall spend in the Cause of Allah, shall be repaid to you, and you shall not be treated unjustly.**

How many terrorists and fundamentalists will appeal to these verses "to strike terror into the hearts of the enemy"?

The majority of the Qur'an's texts themselves clearly identify jihad as physical warfare in Islam. Islamically, Jihad is God's way of establishing the Kingdom of God on earth. Likewise, from the Hadith and the earliest biographies of Muhammad it is just as evident that the early Muslim community understood these Qur'anic texts to be taken literally. Historically, therefore, from the time of Muhammad onwards, jihad was a physical warfare in support of the message of Islam has been a reality for the Muslim community. Hence, it comes as no surprise when the fundamentalists easily appeal to these source materials to justify their actions, not to speak of their teachers who teach the theory and the art of terrorism. This is the reason why the ISIS, the Alqaeda, the Taliban, Hamas, Boko haram and others exist.

Therefore, in the name of spreading the religion, devout Muslim fighters killed millions of people while occupying neighboring Arab lands such as Syria, Palestine, Iraq and non-Arab countries like India, Turkey, Libya, Iran etc. Even Spain had fallen into their hands for hundreds of years. If we are to ask, were these wars defensive? Were those swords used by Islamic soldiers to occupy country after country be considered a symbol of peace and tolerance? Following Muhammad's death, his companions and successors fought each other in relentless savage wars competing for authority.

In summary, Islamic Jihad with the help of Islamic sword– hundreds of tribes were wiped out from the Arabian Peninsula. Thousands were orphaned and widowed. Hazzaz bin Yousuf killed more than a hundred thousand Sahabis, Ibne Khattal was killed in Kaba'a. Later Abdulla Bin Zubair was killed in the same Kaba'a. By the end of the first civil war of Muslims, all the Badari Sahabis were killed. By the end of three civil wars all the Sahabis were killed. Ten thousand Muslims were killed in the Jamal war between Hazrat Ali (RA) and Bibi Ayesha (RA). Islamic scholar Dr. Abu Zayd Shalabi claimed in his book (page-75), in the 'battle of Alees' which took place on the border of Iraq, (Siffin war between Hazrat Ali and Hazrat Mwabia), the Islamic General Khalid killed 70,000 people.

Thousands of non-Muslims were killed. After the death of Prophet Muhammad, there were four most favorite disciples of Prophet who ruled the Islamic kingdom established by the prophet Muhammad, who were known as the most pious caliphs. Out of these four Caliphs—three of them were brutally assassinated, and only one had natural death because of his old age and very short rule of the Islamic state. Karbala was flooded with blood with a roar of "Allahu Akbar!" Was it because of the fact that Islamic sword was the sign of tolerance and peace? The fact of the matter is—sword can never be the sign of peace!

SIDE NOTE:

A friend of mine sent this to me. The original author of it is unknown by yours truly as it was sent to him by someone else who said another person sent it to him and so on. However, you might have come in contact with it, but this is what it reads:
The Muslim is not happy…..
He is not happy in Iran
He is not happy in Iraq
He is not happy in Sudan
He is nor happy in Pakistan
He is not happy in Northern Nigeria
He is not happy in Somalia
He is not happy in Egypt
He is not happy in Syria
He is not happy in Yemen

Where is he happy?
He is happy in the UK
He is happy in the USA
He is happy in Australia
He is happy in France
He is happy in Germany
He is happy in Denmark
He is happy in all the places occupied by the people he calls infidels.
And what does he want to do? He wants to convert the places where he is happy to be like those he is unhappy in.

Islam and Slave-Trade

The world awoke to the shocking news that more than 200 girls were abducted over-night in a remote community called Chibok in Borno state, a predominantly Muslim province in the Northern part of Nigeria at a time when the

Nigerian state was suffering frustration in the hands of the Islamist group; Boko Haram. What will become of these innocent high school girls in the hands of men where kindness is foreign and destruction is as easy as a lion tearing a meat to them? The imagination of the plights of these young school girls in their control was just unbearable and their whereabouts could not be traced by the state. While the world was yet to awake to the reality of such animality, the Islamist leader of the monstrous sect in a released video to the world announced:

"I am the one who captured all those girls and will sell all of them. I have a market where I sell human beings because it is God that says I should sell human beings. Yes I will sell women, because I sell women."

The modern age social media grants one the opportunity to stumble into the reasoning and sentiments of different people around the world. And so, was I opportune to read the responses of some Muslim apologists online as they defended the ridicule and lambaste of the Christians against their religious fundamentalists and their bloody practices. In their defense, the Muslims were saying things like "It is unislamic to engage in slavery", "These are not the teachings of the Prophet Muhammad". Even some Christians in a bid to sound nice and friendly said "My fellow Christians should stop demonizing Islam; these terrorists are not practicing Islam" etc. There is no doubt that a majority of religious people do not know the history and details of their religion and the contents of their so called Holy books. Even if they do and are reminded, they usually pretend that it is a conspiracy or will blatantly excuse it with denial or dishonesty. Some Muslims may quote some few nice lines from the Koran that briefly speaks against such acts but will totally pretend that there are no contradictions in the same book which equally permits the practice of slavery. Allah from his words as depicted in the Koran has exhibited trends of multi-personality disorder. Allah in the Koran shuns slavery in some Ayat (Islamic scripture or verse in the Koran), allows it in another provided slaves are not Arabs, tells men to treat women as part of their body and then tells them to beat them for insubordination, claims that Abraham, David, Joseph, Moses, Jesus were his messengers but commands Muslims to kill their Abrahamic counterparts and then says he hates killing but reserves a special place for killers of kaffirs (also Kuffar meaning unbelievers). Any doubt why his followers are killing each other?

I hate to always do this, but I am always sad and irritated by the deep and lack of information and ignorance by the African especially the religious ones. The truth is that Shekau, the Boko Haram leader is not wrong, he is doing as his religion dictates. Slavery is "HALAL" (lawful) in Islam. A question was asked on a Muslim website:

Q: Can a slave girl be used for prostitution?

This was their answer:

"Sex with slave girls and captured women is halal (lawful) according to ayat 4.3, 4.24, 23.6, 33.52, and 70.30 and many hadiths. However, using them as prostitutes is only allowed if she agrees to it. But if she desires chastity (and likes to restrict sex only with you), you cannot force her. Force is allowed only under compulsion (such as hunger) as the following ayah indicates (same way as Allah had allowed Muslims to use prostitutes with temporary nikah (marriage in Islam) under compulsion):

Qur'an 24:34 says: **"Force not your 'SLAVE-GIRLS' to whoredom (prostitution) if they desire chastity, that you may seek enjoyment of this life. But if anyone forces them, then after such compulsion, Allah is oft-forgiving."**

Correct me if I am wrong but this is what can be deducted from the above verse:

- First of all Slave-girls ownership is legitimate in Islam

-Muslims are allowed to rape prisoners of war. It is halal (lawful) for them.

-But don't force your slave-girl to whoredom. But even if you did, so what, Allah will forgive you any way.

Muslims can trade their slaves for ransom, money, weapons, horses and goods or as a gift. Mohammed practiced this perfectly....

The History of al-Tabari. Vol 8, page 29-30:

"From his share of captive women, prophet gave his son-in-law, Ali a slave girl, Raytah bt Hilal to enjoy her at his will. He also presented Uthman B.Affan, his son-in-law, another slave girl Zainab b. Hayan, and bestowed another girl (name unknown) to his father in-law Omar Ibn Khattab. Omar gave that girl to his son Abdullah.

Most of Muhammad's other elite companions received slave girls as gifts.

Bukhari (34:351) –

"Narrated Jabir bin Abdullah:

A man decided that a slave of his would be manumitted after his death and later on he was in need of money, so the prophet took the slave and said, "Who will buy this slave from me?" Nu'aim bin Abdullah bought him for such and such price and the prophet gave him the slave."

The above account narrates how Muhammad sold a slave for money. He was thus a slave trader.

ISIS in the spirit of this fashion of slave trade emulated their prophet in Iraq. ISIS which appears to be the most brutal group of fundamentalists ever known declared war on the Iraq state and have been unleashing mayhem as they succeed in taking over towns and cities in Iraq in their bid to create an Islamic state. They advanced into the Kurdish region of Iraq, taking over Qaraqosh, a town with large Christian population and Mosul as well. Christians were given an ultimatum to leave, convert to Islam or die (which is mostly done by beheading). After slaughtering thousands of men in their captured towns, the Muslim insurgents captured the women for slavery and displayed their captives for auctioning in the public marketplace. Captured women from Mosul deemed very attractive were taken to ISIS princes to be their personal sex slaves.

When folks like me laugh and say the belief in God is vitriolic and cancerous to the society, God-knowing folks will be going paranoia and calling us "FOOLS". Now look at the fruits and usefulness of believing in God.

"EXTREMISTS HAVE SHOWN WHAT FRIGHTENS THEM MOST: A GIRL WITH A BOOK." - MALALA YOUSAFZAI

Child Marriage and Pedophilia in Islam

Muslims have been given an embarrassment by their prophet Mohammed to constantly defend. While some do not bother making any argument for the child marriage between their prophet and Aisha or Ayesha as recorded in the Koran by equally practicing and engaging in same act. To this set of people, there is no such thing as a pedophile in Islam and it is equally lawful to marry a girl child and of course they are not wrong about this, Islamically. Islam clearly permits pedophilia without any hesitation or shame. The only difference is that pedophilia is called marriage in Islam and therefore it is allowed.

Others bring an embarrassment to themselves by inventing a more embarrassing excuse as a defense for the prophet's action. Pedophilia is an act which in this age will be awarded with a jail term in a saner clime. However, in other climes where Insanity is the decorum like Saudi Arabia, Afghanistan, Pakistan, Iran, etc, such practices are very common. This is what a typical excuse by Muslim apologists about the child bride of Muhammad with Aisha mostly sounds like:

"That in warm climates and 1400 years ago, girls became mature at the age of 6." Yeah right! When one wants to defend insanity, he in turn suffers an infection from insanity. However, this is how one can debunk and answer their absurdity:

I am afraid, but 9-year-old girls in Arabia are still 9-year-old children. Unless the Muslims can advance a scientific evolutionary theory that human race has undergone a huge mutation during these 1400 years and in those days, women reached adulthood at the age of 9. The fact remains that the Prophet had sexual feelings for an underage girl and this was absurd. To be convinced that 9-year-old children were not always children, even during the time of Mohammed, we do not have to look farther than another hadith narrated by Ayesha herself. In the following hadith, Ayesha is revealing that she was playing on a swing when her mother took her to the Prophet:

Sunan Abu-Dawud Book 41, Number 4915, also Number 4915 and Number 4915

"Narrated Aisha, Ummul Mu'minin:

The Apostle of Allah (pbuh) married me when I was seven or six. When we came to Medina, some women came.

According to Bishr's version: **Umm Ruman came to me when I was swinging. They took me, made me prepared and decorated me. I was then brought to the Apostle of Allah (pbuh), and he took up cohabitation with me when I was nine. She halted me at the door, and I burst into laughter."**

She did what every normal girl child will do at her age by playing with dolls:

Sahih Bukhari Volume 8, Book 73, Number 151

Narrated Aisha:

I used to play with the dolls in the presence of the Prophet, and my girl friends also used to play with me. When Allah's Apostle used to enter (my dwelling place) they used to hide themselves, but the Prophet would call them to join and play with me.

NOTE: The playing with the dolls and similar images is forbidden, but it was allowed for 'Aisha at that time, as she was a little girl, not yet reached the age of puberty- (Fateh-al-Bari page 143, Vol.13)

Sahih Muslim Book 008, Number 3327:

'A'isha (Allah be pleased with her) reported that Allah's Apostle (may peace be upon him) married her when she was seven years old, and he was taken to his house as a bride when she was nine, and her dolls were with her; and when he (the Holy Prophet) died she was eighteen years old.

Common sense dictates that if she was still playing with her dolls at that age it should ordinary tell any apologist that she was not mature enough to learn about sex, worst of all, from a man who could be her grandfather. Terrible!

THE RELIGIOUS VIEW OF SIN

Sin is an imaginary offence. It is a self-imposed guilt. What the religious people called SIN is a psychological cage, non-existing crime. Sin is simply going against God's word no matter how good or evil it seems to you or anyone else. For instance, Saul didn't KILL all Amalekites (including women and babies) as God commanded him to do and this action of Saul is considered to be evil and was punished in 1 Sam 15:2-26 of the bible.

Quoting verse 3 of the 1Samuel 15: **"Now go and completely destroy the entire Amalekite nation- men, women, children, babies, cattle, sheep, camel and donkeys"**.

Again, from the fable tales of the Abrahamic books, Abraham who is considered a very righteous man heard the voice of God to kill and sacrifice his only offspring to God, his ability to heed to such an atrocious order is what is considered as righteous and right-standing with God. Assuming he disobeyed the voice and wore his conscience as his sleeves he would have been punished and termed a rebellious, unrighteous and devilish man. The same goes to King David, who was considered as "a man after God's heart". His terrorism in the name of God as highlighted in the bible is second to none. In some instances, he was ordered by the so called God to kill every living thing including women and children and did not disobey. And Kingdom is regarded as a more righteous man than his predecessor Saul who wore his conscience. You should feel abused listening to this type of fairytale labeled righteous if you are reasonable.

Sin in many instances is using your natural reason and conscience to act. The righteous man is the man who does whatever God says irrespective of his conscience and the consequences of his actions. This explains why the jihadist is every enthusiastic to blow himself up in the name of God. To the non-jihadist, it is atrocious, evil and stupid, but to the Jihadist and his word of God, he is doing the work of God and we are the sinners for thinking such of him and he is the righteous man because he'll be rewarded with 72 virgins in heaven.

The definition of sin differs from one religion and sect to the other. In the Islamic version, among other things listed as sinful, the following are stated as the 7 filthiest possible things in Islam (najis):

1. Dogs
2. Pigs
3. Blood
4. Alcohol
5. Cadaver (human or animal)
6. Urine and faeces
7. Non-muslims

The modern Christian believes that marrying more than one wife is sinful and in some sects, divorce is prohibited. But the Muslim is permitted to have up to four wives on earth and 72 more virgins awaiting him in heaven. And there are procedures under Islamic law that allows divorce. While the Christian scoffs at the beliefs of the Muslim at finds him a very sinful and misled man, the Muslim shares the same sentiment when he looks upon the Christian who keeps dogs for pet, eats pork meat and drinks alcohol. He is very certain in his heart that the Christian will burn in hell, especially for not accepting Mohammed as the last prophet of God. The Christian counterpart is more than convinced as written in the bible that the Muslim has not accepted Jesus as the Son of God that he is doomed for eternal torture. To him, the Muslim is an anti-Christ.

But when I look at them both, I shake my head, because rather than bringing meaningful development and peaceful coexistence in the world, they are all constituting nuisance and all manners of social problems with their imaginary offences and delusions of heaven and hell. But then, delusion is comforting to the ignorant and irritating to the knowledgeable.

SIDE NOTE:

I woke up one morning to read this message from a Christian adherent:

"Imoh, the Lord has told me you'll be a leader. The Lord told me you are going to lead in this generation, mark my words, go and write today's date down! But you need to get yourself on the Lord's side to walk in His Grace".

My response: I am grateful to the Lord for designating from his busy schedule to send a message to me through you. I am feeling awesome on mental erection right now, for he abandon His attention from pressing issues like Somalia, Niger, Mali, Northern Nigeria, millions of sick patients all over the world to deliver such an orgasm of a news to me. He must have searched for me but couldn't find me to deliver such a message. Just like in the Garden of Eden he must have screamed "Son of David where are you?" But the 1 billion plus human population filtered the voice from reaching my geographical coordinates. I am really honored, to hear this. Tell him his message is well received here alongside His other messages like "Jesus is coming SOON", "The Lord never fails", "When you call, I'll answer", "Righteousness exalts a Nation", etc and the reputation of these messages inscrutably precedes this one.

"If there is a God who will damn his children forever, I would rather go to hell than to go to heaven and keep the society of such an infamous tyrant. I make my choice now. I despise that doctrine. It has covered the cheeks of this world with tears. It has polluted the hearts of children and poisoned the imaginations of men....

What rights have you, sir, Mr. Clergyman, you minister of the gospel to stand at the portals of the tomb, at the vestibule of eternity, and fill the future with horror and fear? I do not believe this doctrine, neither do you. If you did, you could not sleep one moment. Any man who believes it, and has within his breast a decent, throbbing heart, will go insane. A man who believes that doctrine and does not go insane has a heart of a snake and the conscience of a hyena"- Robert Green Ingersoll

THE AFTER LIFE GIBBERISH

In his desire to convince this Son of David right here about the existence of heaven and hell and all the afterlife gobbledygook, a Christian acquaintance asked me "so where do you think you'll be after you pass away?" "The same place I was before my parents had intercourse", I replied. It's funny how the religious care so much about an afterlife without occurring to them that once upon a time there was zero and nothingness aka "BEFORELIFE". When you disassemble a piano, where does the music go?

After-life is analogous to before-life. Anyone who wants to make a big deal out of the after-life chimera should first of all explain where he was before-life. If he cannot provide a reasonable response, such an individual should be passed for a quixotic jackass. More ridiculous is the individual who tells the other he will be punished eternally because of some "original sin". A god that is happy to condemn me to hell for not believing in him because he has refused to proof his existence or for some other petty reasons, but he'll comfortably open his residence for baby rapists, murderers, terrorists, homicidal maniacs, if they simply utter a line of allegiance to his existence, is not the type of god anyone should be proud to sell to anyone.

I threw a question out of curiosity to this so called spiritual brother. You know

the type that is almost 2nd in command to the Holy Spirit, who knows God so much that even God would have to ask the brother to clarify some things about

Himself. Yeah, that kind of brother who has his name definitely under the pillow of God.

The question was this "If Abacha, Adolf Hitler, Idi Amin, and other genocidal maniacs, etc (at that time we did not have terrorists who blow themselves up with bombs to be included in the question)- If these guys at their few seconds to death accept Jesus, will they make heaven?

It was a pure question of innocence. But the brother shocked me saying:

"No matter how evil, murderous and disastrous a person can be, if in his death bed he utters a simple line of 'Jesus come into my life', that he is making heaven straight-up."
"What about the poor starving people in Somalia, Niger, Mali etc who have suffered so much and have done no

harm to anyone on earth, will they go to hell if they do not believe in Jesus even if nobody told them about him?"

His reply, "Yes! They will go to hell. And that is why we must preach the gospel to them."

"So if someone murders my father and Mum and probably me, you mean he can go to heaven even when my murdered people did not do any evil at all and I could go to heaven and meet the murderers of my parents while my parents are in hell?" I asked to be sure again. "Yes", he replied sternly.

That was the day I nailed the final good bye to such a cold-blooded, unjustified looney.

Even if that place is real, I do not desire the company of criminals, killers, rapists, genocidal maniacs. If I am getting the same reward with such monsters while those who did not come any close to their turpitude are going to be tortured, then something is wrong

with the person who rewards them and punishes their victims. The whole thing reads like the memoirs of Homer Simpson.

The idea that a benevolent deity would punish all humanity for two people eating a fruit is not reconcilable with benevolence or wisdom. The same sky-character is said to have drowned all his creations including babies and animals because there was too much of sin. But despite all these killings, he still hasn't forgiven mankind for their progenitor eating this fruit, so he decides the best way to forgive us is to kill his son who cannot die. And we are told to be grateful for this odious tripe and shouldn't question it either or we'll be roasted in a celestial oven for eternity. Can anyone see any difference between this and the imaginations of a demented patient? It is a good thing we know it is false. The Abrahamic Omni-janitor is not a pleasant character at all.

How the primitive writers of the bible were able to reconcile punishment for eating a fruit, a flood to drown all and sundry, killing your child in order to forgive your other children with benevolence is beyond my comprehension. It is enough to make Homer Simpson feel like a genius but they then say if you don't accept this dumb story as true, you will be thrown into a universal oven for eternity; you simply have to laugh at the idiocy of it all when people in the 21st century believe these tales and insist that you must join them in their inebriation for this hokum or face being exterminated by sky-daddy.

I am usually baffled when a believer says that one denies his Abrahamic literature simply because he wants an excuse to engage in immorality and their concocted sin. You'll find them say things like: "atheists and unbelievers are simply people who do not want to believe in the bible so that they can give themselves an excuse to live a sinful life." Out of curiosity, I do ask them: "are you believing in the bible because you want to give yourself an excuse to live a sinful life against the commandments of the Koran?" If you are a Christian and you eat pork, drink alcohol, keep dogs for pets, and of course deny the prophet-hood of Mohammed, are you not aware that you have been prescribed to burn in an eternal hell by the Koran? So you are telling me that you are disbelieving Islam and the Koran because you want to excuse yourself in committing Islamic sins?

According to them, one who chooses to be irreligious does so because he wants to freely practice sin. In other words, they are saying that their spurious belief in incoherent myths and tales of an afterlife is the reason why they are moral and good. I have equally heard some say that one chooses atheism and religion disbelief because he is unhappy with life due to his refusal to believe in the God tale. I am stunned by this type of religious psychological imagination. Anyone who considers himself happy with

185

this type of reasoning, I must confess has my envy on how they've found equanimity and solace in their level of brilliance. My envy is redolent of the same envy I am engrossed with when I look upon a pig finding great comfort and luxury in dirt and mud. Perhaps I may consider the pig pitiable while finding great recreation in mud, and I'm sure the pig will return the favor and look pitifully on me like one who knows no happiness and lacks wisdom. Truly, reasoning is to the religious what God is to the atheist.

A reasonable human does not need the promise of Heaven and the threat of eternal damnation to engage in good deeds and adopt empathy. Anyone who claims to be good and professes empathy due his/her patronage of some spurious belief is simply being good under duress and pretence. And I find it laughable that a God can be hoodwinked into inhabiting with people who are acting the script of his totalitarian compulsion to please his fancies. The idea of a morality based on a promise of a reward or fear of punishment is indeed laughable. True morality does not require a reward. Kindness is its own reward. It is obvious that the goal of these Bronze Age fairy tales was simply to use fear as a recruiting tool.

You simply have to be sheepish to swallow all the bunk about humanity being punished because a talking snake told a woman to eat a fruit and then some sky genie decides to kill his immortal son in order to forgive said sins. It all sounds like a script written by Homer Simpson.

The idea of vicarious redemption is in itself repugnant and then you have to attempt to reconcile original sin with any notion of benevolence and wisdom. Why would a father punish his grand children and great grand children? Most human beings are not this malicious to their offspring but we are asked to believe that the Jewish sky boss that is regarded as the creator of the Cosmos did these things and he is absolutely merciful.

Anyway, I have risen above fear and choose to be logical, skeptical and apply my reason (which some may claim that this same God gave us). I'd rather be good and sincere to myself and humanity than live in delusions and fear of some imaginary Hell and devils. And I'd continue to speak out when the chance presents itself.

SIDE NOTE:

PARODY OF HEAVEN AND HELL

Oprah Winfrey: doesn't believe that Jesus is the ONLY way to God, not married, built charity schools like the one in South Africa for girls who can't afford education and it's for free, and has donated millions to the homeless and disaster victims. **DESTINATION:** HELL

The Popular Nigerian Preacher, Bishop David: owns 2 private universities with high school fees, preacher of gospel, expelled a lot of students from his school on the grounds of "smoking, not going to church, owning mobile phones, watching porn, etc", slapped a poor lady for saying "I'm a witch for Christ". **Destination:** HEAVEN

Nigerian Celebrity Preacher, Pastor Chris Okotie: preacher of the bible, divorcee par-excellence, claimed that God asked him to contest for the presidency in Nigeria and lost woefully. **Destination:** Heaven

Andrew Carnegie: Atheist, founder of the Carnegie steel company now the US Steel, industrialist and employer of labour, arguably the greatest philanthropist in his time. **Crime:** does not believe in God, in his words: "I don't believe in God. My god is patriotism. Teach a man to be a good citizen and you have solved the problem of life." ~ Andrew Carnegie. **DESTINATION:** HELL FIRE

Mahtma Ghandi: Not a Christian, in his words: "If 'atheist' means 'someone who is not superstitious', then I'm a 'super atheist". An Apostle of peace, a peaceful activist, philanthropist to the core. **Crime:** Not a Christian or Muslim, in his words "I like your Christ, I don't like your Christians, your Christians are unlike your Christ". **Destination**: HELL FIRE

Osama Bin Laden, Al Qaeda, Hezbollah, ISIS, Boko Haram and Jihadists: Firm believers of Allah, responsible for deaths of thousands non-Muslims and Muslims alike, anti-education, anti- women, terrorists. **Destination**: HEAVEN with 72 virgins for a well done job on earth

Ellen De Generes: Lesbian, generous, employer of labour, philanthropist. **Crime**: LESBIANISM. **Destination**: HELL FIRE

Christian Sister, Victoria: Churchgoer, speaks in tongues, knows more than 1,000 bible passages, slept with her pastor aka "Daddy-In-The-Lord" and other married men then attributes money given to her by the men as "Blessings from God", activist and lover of Jesus, dislikes atheists and unbelievers like Imoh "Son of David". **Destination:** HEAVEN

Imoh David: lover of fine wine, antique, art, women, books and luxury. Ambitious, bold, curious, business-minded, lover of fine women, idealist, not convicted of a crime, sarcastic, outspoken, unconventional. **DESTINATION:** ???????

No God worth the name would espouse belief over good deeds. Belief is not a virtue but good deeds are. We are asked to believe that some God would roast a good Hindu man in his celestial oven for not believing in him even though he created him to be born there in the first place. This of course will reasonable to you if you believe that the bloodthirsty entity in the book of talking snakes is the Creator of the cosmos. The ideology is insane and completely lacking in benevolence and wisdom.

Why Would A Perfect God Create Imperfect Humans and Then Punish Them For Erring?

END-TIME AND JUDGEMENT DAY

If I wanted to control a mass of ignorant sheep herding desert folks, I would invent a story about a terrible ending of their lives if they do not do as they are told.

I am always very afraid and occupied with the grieve of discomfort when a Christian uses the word "SOON" for a future arrangement. I am very scared of the word SOON when uttered from the lips of a Christians. I can't help my malaise for this circumstance which is bore out of an authentic disturbing reputation with regards to the word SOON in the perception of the Christian. SOONOPHOBIA; permit me to invent the word to suit my malady.

Christians do not know what SOON entails. Religion makes people out of touch with reality and reasoning without them knowing. If you have been saying something will happen SOON before the 14th century and now in 2014 you still carry-over the term SOON for the same expectation while awaiting its manifestation, it is obvious that you are ridiculing yourself. And out of nicety and in the spirit of amorous samaritanism we should amend the definition of SOON to appease the Christian's ad infinitum expectation.

"SOON" is simply a word used in postponing your embarrassment to the grave and passing the baton to the posterity, who will in turn nurse same embarrassment to another set of unsuspecting hopefuls.

I don't know why people still hold the fancy view and pious fear of End time. When you ask an "end time" monger, they won't fail to fill your ears with the news of earth-quakes, plane crashes, wars, etc. This is what happens when people are taught Abrahamic curriculums in school rather than science subjects.

Anyone who was taught Geography in school should understand the causes of earth quakes, and other natural disasters. But even if you were not taught, such information of simple scientific explanation is fraught everywhere; for starters use a search engine and bail yourself from myths. In this age where information has no hiding place and the libraries are freely open, it is unforgiveable to market tales of natural disasters as some divine syndrome of an "end".

There is no such thing as an end time. Time has no end! Put your mind to rest. Wars did not begin today. As a matter of fact your "end time" literature has contributed to almost all wars fought in recorded history of mankind, and time has not ended. From the earliest battles in ancient Mesopotamia till today's wars of Israel and Palestine. Since the dawn of time war has always had a significant place in history. And people mostly fought over nonsense. Let me give you a rundown of some wars in mankind's history:

When Napoleon was on conquest he launched what became the Napoleonic wars (1803- 1815). Guess what, your sky crew back then called him the anti-Christ and the beast and all that. That one passed.

We had the Spanish-American War in 1898. The still cried end time and it passed.

World War 1 came. They cried end-time.

Adolf Hitler was dissatisfied with the outcome so he began his own. He was believed with certainty to be the much expected anti-Christ with the 666 mark. That one passed again.

The Vietnam War came, they said the same thing.

George Bush came at Iraq. Christians in America and other parts of the world were certain that he was the anti-Christ.

Now they say is Barrack Obama. We know he'll soon pass the baton to another person you people will deem fit to appoint as your new anti-Christ.

Meanwhile, other Christian sects have been accusing all the popes and the Catholic Church to be the anti-Christ. I even read a Christian conspiracy theorist who said the black pope will be the anti-Christ, and we all know that the conspiracist is never lacking in evidence to support any claims even if he claims that the Mona Lisa portrait was painted by Jesus Christ. Even the pop singer Lady Gaga was not spared from the anti-Christ label. Chris Angel, Christopher Hitchens, Richard Dawkins, Sam Harris, George Carlin, Bertrand Russell, etc are all anti-Christs, damn! What I do not understand is whether the anti-Christ is a single person or a generously shared title. Labeling a person an anti-Christ is not anymore remarkable than labeling a person an anti-Harry Potter.

This week the NASA spacecraft landed on Pluto and it has been sending images of the planet back. and also, this same week a "BORN AGAIN" Christian woman in Africa landed in hell and got messages from Gaddafi and Whitney Houston. science and religion made a trip somewhere.

The difference is that when science sends an object or life form on an exploration or expedition, it reports back with evidence like images and video recordings. But when delusion and schizophrenia proudly sponsored by religion sends a religitard on a journey or exploration, they come back with fantastic narration good enough from a donkey's butt-hole.

If I were to lend a word of encouraging advice of practice to the believers, when next one of your sky-partners embarks on a trip to your celestial Eldorado and Halloween oven, connect a photo printer or a live podcast to him or her. Who wouldn't love to see the horror chambers of hell? The Gadaffi and Whitney Houston we know are not camera shy. well, I have my own share of story:

Last night I was with Thor in Valhalla but the gates of Valhalla read "No cameras allowed", and so, no group selfie for me. At least I understand you guys very well than everyone; espirit de corps!

Evidence is a contraband in religion but the arrogance of assertion is a gospel right, legitimate, we are!

When will the religious ever stop carrying-over this endless history of end-time delusion and the anti-Christ paranoia? 2014 and you are still shopping for an anti-Christ and certain about an end-time? Sometimes, I am jealous of your delusions.

One popular verbiage that one would lost count of from the lips of the so called believer is "God has not given us the spirit of fear" and then the other "I shall not die". Many other rhetoric of fear is plenty but these two seem to top the chart.

I do not understand how people who speak highly of a place with streets of gold and mansions allocated per citizen, and most importantly, the ambience is devoid of war, famine, crime, disasters, etc would devote 80% of their prayer lyrics against death- the one and only bridge that transits them to their celestial nation. I wish I understand how and why it is so.

The believer panics at the mention of the word "death". "God forbid!" they will thunder whenever a thing arouses the imagination of death in their cognition. and of course, they never fail to hastily wish death on their perceived enemies. Death, is a dire punishment and disgrace to them.

But yet, they assert that when they die, it awaits for them joy and merriment. To die however, they wish it not upon themselves and entertain no such imagination whether in humor or ordeal. What possible can be defined of this?

Nobody carries so much insecurity, fear and hate like the diehard churchgoer . they are afraid of almost everything and everyone around them. "This world is evil", they chant. But you folks occupy the world of the greatest in number, who then makes it evil? I wonder. If it is evil, why then do you pray to your sky-daddy to extend your tenancy?

The rate at which the apostles of life after death and candidates of sky palace pray against death is alarming even to whom they pray to. About to board a bus, they pray against accident, on a flight, they pray against plane crash, in the church, they cast and bind untimely death. In fact to die early is an agony in the mind of the believer of life after death. How can anyone dislike any circumstance that will unite them with their father? You don't love your father or you do not like where he stays, or maybe you subconsciously do not believe he exists. These are the best possible answers I can conjure in a brief second of amusement.

I think sky-daddy will be feeling very bad each time he hears his people pray to him to cancel any situation that will lead them to him. It is not their fault, dear sky-daddy. In the sub-consciousness of the believer lies a picture of a boring opera-styled dirge environment with no cable TV, no I-pads, no Facebook, Instagram and Twitter, no cars but horses, donkeys and most importantly, endless days of singing boring dirge lyrics to a white-bearded man on a throne for eternity. No holidays, that is boring, dearest sky-daddy. Who will love such a place? no wonder they do not want to die.

Their preachers even take it further by securing themselves with bullet proof cars and armed guards in other to prevent any situation that can send them to the company of sandals-wearing men like Peter and Paul or goat-skin couture men like John the Baptist and Elijah, men with beards that haven't been shaved for centuries. Islam was smart to add virgins so that it can be libido enticing. Too bad the Romans failed to conceive such a holy pornography.

Believing in life after death and then praying against death is like going to school and refusing to graduate and doing everything possible to remain in school but at the same time telling everyone that the life of a graduate is better than that of a student

The three Abrahamic religions unanimously agree in the assertion of the "end time" and a judgment day albeit their standards and description of the end and that of the judgment day differ. Besides their assertions being starry-eyed and redolent of childish superstition, if going by the standards of their holy books, you'll readily entertain yourself with their inability to spot their religious dichotomy. Say God exists; evil exists because God allowed it. Assuming to be true that their holy books are infallible and the accounts therein are pardoned for some moments to be plausible, the Abrahamic God (Yahweh, Allah, Jehovah, etc) lacks the moral locus standi to be a judge and adjudicator of wrong doings or sin or whatever their fantasy calls it. The account in their books has stated clearly that the master-craft of evil is him (God). By their account, man did not create evil, their god is the creator of evil and their imaginary enemy; Satan or whatever. Starting with the crimes of killing, he is countlessly guilty of the following:

genocide, homicide, episcopicide (the killing of bishops or priests), ecocide (the destruction of nature or ecosystem), aborticide (killing of festus or unborn babies), femicide (killing of women), gynaecide, infanticide (killing of children), parasuicide (an attempted murder), senicide (killing of old men), suicide (killing of self), filicide (killing of one's own child), vaticide (killing of prophets), and even the inconsequential like bovicide (killing of cattle and farm animals).

As a matter of fact, he is an OMNI-CIDE. The Abrahamic god is guilty of treachery and deception. For example, the Quran calls Allah a *"makr"* (*Makr* means the practice of guile and deception), in fact the Koran describes Allah as the best makr there is:

"But they (the Jews) were deceptive, and Allah was deceptive, for Allah is the best of deceivers (Wamakaroo wamakara Allahu waAllahu khayru al-makireena)!" S. 3:54; cf. 8:30.

Likewise in the bible: **Ezekiel 14:9: And if the prophet be deceived when he hath spoken a thing, I the LORD have deceived that prophet, and I will stretch out my hand upon him, and will destroy him from the midst of my people Israel.**

Besides being adulterous, he abused his office and "OMNINESS", by using his power to sleep with another man's wife to give birth to his son; Jesus. He is biased, corrupt, and has created so much chaos with his nepotism e.g. encouraging his other children (Israelites and Arabs) to enslave and kill his other children or creations and then take their wives and marry.

His modus Vivendi is that of a jealous, insecure, dangerous, arrogant and destructive narcissist. While tagging people like this Son of David right here SINNERS and liable to be attacked by the heavenly arsenal aka wrath of God. He is keeping mute and giving a blind eye to the countless sufferings of children and mankind, and the con-men and religious leaders are deceiving people on the pulpit. His sebastomaniac children are bombing his other children with his name as he observes with comforting silence, but he'll take delight in finding people like me offensive and the most heinous of all, how bold and fair of him. And to crown it, he has refused to proof himself and declare which religion is true and false (maybe he is camera shy) but in the end he'll come back and punish people for his failures and inability to put his creatures or creations in order. He is the "OMNI" of all evils and the most repugnant of demeanor. It is man who has the locus standi to judge God and not the other way round. The good thing is that he is imaginary.

The all powerful and all knowing Jewish genie allows his favourites to be enslaved and then decides he wants to free them. "Why does he need pharaoh's permission to free them if he is omnipotent?" you might ask. This Jewish God who claims to be benevolent then proceeds to embark on a game of celestial foreplay by hardening Pharaoh's heart when he agrees to free his pets. This demented desert deity then proceeds to slaughter children and animals when Pharaoh does precisely what hardening his heart would make him do. We are told that this story demonstrates Yahweh's power and signs. This senseless slaughter of children is celebrated as "Passover" amongst the fans of Yahweh .This insane display of inhumanity is what is deemed divine. This is one of the clearest examples of the surrender of reason, empathy and humanity that is required to be religious. Is it not a good thing we know this disgusting and odious bunk is just a myth?

"Religion in all its expressions is the vilest form of unreason!" Richard Dawkins merely highlighted one of the numerous fabulous inanities in the Judeo-Christianity ideology; inanities also sufficiently present in Islam. How do you love man so much and still consecrate one race as your "chosen" people, yet you stood idly by while an Arian racist slaughtered 6million of them. But again, I don't want to expend otherwise useful verbiage on the alleged actions or inactions of a being who is famed to possess omnipotence, omniscience, and omnipresence, but 'created' a world where the ground opens up to swallow innocent babies, delivering them up to molten fire in the earth's core.

If this deity truly exists, I do not blame him for hiding. When you possess this kind of history and reputation of character, celestial exile is the most honourable thing to accord yourself. If he exists, he still has a lot of amends to do showing himself. The day he musters the confidence to show up the way he allegedly did to the Judeo-Christian-Islam Abraham and Moses, we may consider taking him seriously by engaging him with questions, but until then, he must be regarded as a character of literature; a fraudulent craftsmanship of iron-age jingoism.

If God wants us to believe in him and follow any particular religion by FAITH, then he shouldn't have given us a mind capable of logic and critical reasoning.

SIDE NOTE:

The theist and religious may in their customary routine find it desirous to appraise the sky-daddy on their birthdays; in fact some of them do that every day, owing it pledgeful to thank some God as a gratitude for bestowing life on them. Their plight, I understand very well, for in my times of "religitardness", I thought same, but now, I am free from such idiosyncrasy.

Many will consider themselves very BLESSED or recipient of some kind of GRACE, BENEVOLENCE and MERCY from whatever they consider as God. This indeed, I thought as much when my senses was under the administration of indoctrination and fable tales.

Contrary to what the religious thinks of his being alive, the truth is that being alive is a CURSE; a burden of the flesh. Better is the unborn than the born or the living. Even the dead are better than the living. The be alive is a burden; the burden of paying bills, the burden of working hard, the burden of gossip, the burden of prayers, the burden of hopes/wishes and disappointments, the burden of sickness and escaping death, the burden of enmity, etc. While the living is on the conscious fight of trying to postpone his death sentence, he doesn't want to come to terms with the reality that being alive is like being a criminal whose death sentence is pending and could be decided anytime and anywhere.

The religious more than anyone else is convinced that his being alive is indeed a gift from some God. This indeed is a misconception from medieval consciousness and mentality of religious indoctrination. How can you call something that would be taken from you willy-nilly a gift? This is a skew-whiff understanding of what a gift is. A thing is considered a "GIFT" if it's yours forever. If you claim someone gave something to you as a gift, and then he'll come back later to take it from you, how is that a gift? The foremost characteristic and attribute of a GIFT is that the recipient of this GIFT has autonomy over this said GIFT, but if you ask the believer he'll assert "MY LIFE IS OWNED BY GOD". If your life is owned by a God, how does that make your life a GIFT from God? The notion is irreconcilable.

"There is no greater happiness than freedom from Worry, and there is no greater wealth than contentment" says Lao Tsu. Who is truly a man of contentment, great happiness and free from worry? If you ask this Son Of David here, I'll give it you succinctly that the unborn and the dead are truly the happiest of all, for they are free from worry and are absolutely contented in their state, for there is no greater wealth than this.

I have no deity to thank, other than nature. I did not ask to be born, neither did I apply for life on earth, if at all there is a God that is responsible of my being, he owes me an apology for bringing me here without my consent, for sending me to this place under duress and without sheer negotiation with me. So what the heck do you mean by I should be grateful to someone who I haven't seen and whose name has caused more mishap than cocaine? He should have said to me "Hey Son of David, do you want to be born a Nigerian, do you want to be born in the 1980s, do you want to be born tall, short, fat, Hindu, etc? He sent me here without my consultation, approval and consent. In real sense, if that God you people refer to exists, he owes me apologies and payment of damages in excesses than I owe him thanks.

Well, I am here now on this planet, so I'll do the best of my living to the uttermost surfeit of my essence. I live life creatively and make an art out of my existence. In the words of the US cartoonist Scott Adams: "Creativity is allowing yourself to make mistakes. Art is knowing which ones to keep". Succinctly, I make art out of life.

"Hey Son of David how dare you say that! You have blasphemed against God, blah blah blah..." the religious may say. Bertrand Russell said "... And if there were a God, I think it very unlikely that He would have such an uneasy vanity as to be offended by those who doubt His existence". It's not "god" that will take offense to what I've said it always humans. And here is another one to the religious: "If there is a god maybe it rewards those who don't believe on the basis of insufficient evidence and punishes those who do." ~ Peter Boghossian.

"Son of David why is that you like saying these things against God and religion?" The irritated may ask. Well, this is why: My friend, I don't know how to pretend, that is a fault from God (if you claim he created me)! I never wanted to be irreligious or an unbeliever, I just wanted to read the bible, Koran and all the so called holy books then applied my common sense, well, here I am.

"Everything God has made has a crack"~Ralph Waldo Emerson. So if you claim God made me and knew me before I was conceived, I think he already knew that this Son of David right here will be this way, so he loves me the way I am, after-all you claim he knows the end from the beginning. Well, it's a good thing that he is an alter-ego of you.

When they came, they brought "holy books" which they claimed was written or revealed by "God". The people they gave the books later became more fanatical than those who gave them the books till today.

DIFFERENCE BETWEEN A FOREIGN DEBATE AND DEBATE FROM RELIGIOUS NIGERIANS

The most frustrating thing any reasonable and irreligious person can embark on is debating with the religious individual. I know particularly about my religious countrymen; they are the most original sample of frustrating it is to debate with the highly religious. Debating with the religious is like playing a game of chess with a crocodile and presenting something logical and factual to them is like reciting poetry to a donkey. Expecting something rational from a religitard is like expecting crude oil from a coconut fruit. Reasoning is far away from the religious as the North Pole is far away from the South Pole. A few of them who try to put up an intellectual debate often display gross chicanery and illogical denial. Their drive from intellectual dishonesty often leads them to invent crude lies and weak concoction to sustain their ailing absurdities.

Debating with religious people can make overrate his brilliance. If you are in a habit of playing soccer with chickens, you can be deceived to assume you are a talented soccer player. Another thing debating with a religitard will get you is irritation. If you are bored about being happy, one way to certainly switch emotions is to debate the religitard. The religitard is one who has divorced his sense of reasoning. To demand reasoning with him is like demanding a divorced man to recall his estranged wife; one whom he has nothing to do with. You are only inviting trouble to yourself. Finally, debating the religious can be a means of entertaining yourself in the absence of humor. Religion is a joke gone bad and taken too seriously by the audience. I find it very anti-social on the part of religion and the religious to be unable tolerate the laughter it offers to its audience. It is very selfish to crack a joke and not allow others to exercise response. I mean, it just unfair to crack a joke and be offended that your humour was well received. I pray the religious will repent from this someday and get themselves some humour kits.

Here is an example of what debating with religious Nigerians is like against debating with the irreligious Europeans on a social media:

European Debate:

Anyone that believes in the biblical stories is a joker! There is no scientific evidence that snakes talked in prehistoric times. Characters like Moses and the stories behind him neither have historical roots nor archeological prove. The Egyptians never at anytime in their historical documentary narrated that such an individual contacted the Pharaoh or Ramsees at the time and the excavation at the red sea has shown that the claims of how the Egyptian army got swallowed in the sea never took place.

European responses:

*James Silva: contrary to your post here is a link to show you a recent excavation at the red sea www.ghstj.com.

*Sarah Water: An ancient writing found by Prof. Luke of North Carolina University has shown the biblical stories where copied from the ancient Aramaic mythology.

*Jane Cole: I disagree with you. The Cairo museum has in display ancient war metals liken to chariots which were found in a town near the Red sea. These metals are equivalent to components of one of the dynasties of Pharaoh III which was about that time.

*Barry Black: This is true, I have made all my archeological research on this topic and everything points to the fact that it never existed.

*Mary Barney: I have always said the bible is an allegory and must not be taken for a historical book. Nice job.

Nigeria (Imoh David):

Anyone that believes in the biblical stories is a joker! There is no scientific evidence that snakes talked in prehistoric times. Characters like Moses and the stories behind him neither have historical roots nor archeological prove. The Egyptians never at anytime in their historical documentary narrated that such an individual contacted the Pharaoh or Ramsees at the time and the excavation at the red sea has shown that the claims of how the Egyptian army got swallowed in the sea never took place.

Religious Nigerians responses:

*Chubike: Signs of the end times.

*Dayo Muyiwa : You are a big Fool! May God punish you.

*Nkiru Joy: May God forgive you, you don't know what you are talking about.

*Idris Kunle : This is one of the reasons Boko Haram said Western education is bad. Too much of book makes someone stupid!

*Funmi Leye: I don't blame you at all, you better go and find something do with your life.

*Funke Olawale: How dare you question God?!

*David Joseph: Imoh you have sold your soul to the Devil to gain fame.

*Richard Oke: all these Christians here you people are stupid! Can't you people prove him otherwise?

*Olaniyi Popoola: you are the anti-Christ, I am deleting you from my friends list.

*Amaka Achebe: Ask the Holy Spirit to direct you! You need deliverance!

*Emmanuel: Imoh what happened to you? You were once the nice church guy I use to know is everything alright?

*Juliet Adesuwa: Why do you post such things in a public forum?

Sunny: Na you go school pass? Idiot! ("na you go school pass?"- A Nigerian Pidgin English which translates "Are you the most educated?"*

> "It should be added that in general, it is the character of every metaphysical and theological argument to seek to explain one absurdity by another"- Michael Bakunin

THE RELIGIOUS AND THEIR DEFENSE:

When debating with Christians I have come to notice a strange dichotomy at work. As they debate with their knowledge of the bible and information that they believe proves their argument they will often resort to a phrase that contradicts the basic premise of their attempt to convince the unbeliever to change mind. When they are faced with an obvious contradiction or lack of rational explanation they say things like "you need the holy spirit to understand these things". The Holy Spirit is an imaginary being, besides; I always wonder if the only talent and skill the Holy Spirit possesses is just to interpret the bible, for I am yet to see any invention on earth that could be ascribed to the craftsmanship of this Holy Spirit. Oh! I forgot, the bible is one. What the apologist actually means is that the unbeliever should be taking his arguments by faith and burying reason. Belief without evidence is called faith. Belief against the evidence is called delusion.

If you spend time as an apologist using the claims and purported history from your holy books to make your arguments and then at the same time ignore evidence or deny the palpable logical conclusion from facts, you are doing nothing but being delusionary to yourself. Affirmation without evidence is delusion, they say.

Being an ardent user of the social media most especially Facebook, the popular evangelist Ray Comfort was asked this question:

QUESTION: Why did God allow sin to be inheritable?

Ray Answers: He allowed sin to be inherited because it was His plan to disallow it through the new birth. The moment we repent and trust in the Savior, God forgives our sins (which are many) gives us an inheritance in Christ, and grants us the gift of everlasting life. If we prefer to stay in our sins we inherit death and ultimately Hell. Now you have your answer.

This is so funny an answer. In other words he is saying: God allowed it so that he could disallow it. That is, God conspired against you so that he can set you free, very comic! When you convince gullible people you have all the answers, you just have to keep up appearances. The real answer is that the people who wrote the bible allowed sin to be inherited so that they could indoctrinate children into their religion from birth. They are simply giving people imaginary offences and guilt so that they can sell them a bail or remedy; very awesome!

When one analysis the errors and the inconsistencies in the bible to a Christian believer, his/her initial response would be that of a cognitive dissonance but in some cases some will opt to the bible passage that says: "For the foolishness of God is wiser than man's wisdom…." This to me is very senseless and pure escapism into greater folly. Foolishness is foolishness; you cannot be hiding under religious beliefs to excuse folly like agreeing the earth is flat, that a talking snake deceived a naked woman in the garden as the raison d'etre of human sufferings, including painful birth and snakes crawling on the ground, that the entire earth was covered by a flood and all the animal species on earth fit into one boat, that it is rational to sacrifice your son to save your other children from a punishment and crime you personally condemned them to.

How can an omniscient God be foolish and say unintelligible things? Listen to the excuse he is giving: "I am being a FOOLISH so that rational humans won't comprehend me". Hello! Who is he (God) competing with? The so called word of God isn't some rocket science, quantum or Astro-physics; man has conquered rocket science and keeps accomplishing greater things. Let me ask, can your word of God reduce the price of gas? What is even more foolish is anyone quoting the foolishness acknowledgement and masturbating his blindness with it.

When one points out the monstrous atrocity committed by God, the believer will either say "You don't question God", or come up with some impassive rhetoric to uphold the actions of an imaginary being as correct, for example, they'll say "He had to defend and protect the children of Israel and bring discipline for breaking the law". It beats me how anyone can comfortably give a blind eye to an outright atrocity in the name of FEAR OF GOD. What kind of father kills his other children to satisfy his one child? Some of them argue, saying "That was in the Old Testament when the law was sacrosanct; if you sin against God, you must be punished! That is why Christ came to die, to take away the curse of the LAW and give us salvation. This also is a ridicule of itself. So in other words, God was an illiterate before, so he suddenly realized and repented of his barbarism. This is to say that he (God) became civilized and more cultured after centuries of engaging in divine primitivism or should I say Omni-barbarism? Doesn't the bible say that "God is the same, yesterday, today and forever" and also "He changes not"? If we should allow this thought for a second, may I ask, what about the damages from his untamed temperament and costly illiteracy; who will pay for it? Highly hilarious beyond the words of my expression. Religion is the best excuse people give themselves in other to make violence and murder sound holy.

> "Philosophy is questions that may never be answered. Religion is answers that may never be questioned." - Anonymous

The stories associated with King David are atrocious and repugnant to a humane mind because of it is devoid of moral justification. How any rational, just, kind-hearted being would read these preposterously repugnant stories, without finding them utterly distasteful, beats me hollow!

King David was an adulterous, genocidal, homicidal maniac who slept with his neighbour's wife, impregnated her, and had his neighbour gruesomely murdered in order to steal his wife. But what was his punishment? The product (baby) of that adulterous affair was killed; and David's wives (polygamy) were cursed to commit adultery. But the evil King David was let alone, and had his sins forgiven. Sounds legit and logical? "Thou shall not kill and commit adultery", I thought that was the commandment?

Then onto the despicable and out of taste story of 70, 000 innocent human beings massacred because King David carried out a census! Now, if King David was the offender (sinner) in carrying out a census, shouldn't King David be the one to pay for his sins? But here we have 70, 000 creatures, among them babies were killed for the crime of King David- "conducting a census". And the murders were only stopped when King David made "animal sacrifice" to appease God! And I thought they said animal sacrifice is the tenet of idol-worshiping pagans? Stupidity is envious when you look at it afar. It takes one who is passionately insincere, block-headed to genocide and violence to deliberately see no evil in this tripe. Truly, a believer is an

209

inane personality. It takes a lot of dishonesty of ethics and snobbery of reason to be religious. It is only the mentally unremorseful that can reconcile comfort with this tale. Stupidity is seeing the obvious and still believing a lie.

There is no face-saving excuse religion can shop for itself in this new age of information and science. I was unfortunate to stumble upon an excuse a religious apologist, who in their characteristic desire to rescue their asses from cognitive dissonance argued that religion brought education and science into the world. He even went ahead to enumerate that the Catholic missionary built schools in Africa and parts of the world. I cannot ascertain whether or not the individual was being willfully dishonest of or it was mere expression of self from ignorance.

Religion never supported science and enlightenment even till date, because it survives and thrives on the ignorance and gullibility of people. If people start thinking and being enlightened, who will believe their twaddle? There is a timeline in earth's history called "THE DARK AGES". It is not called DARK AGES because there was no electricity or power supply, it earned its name because it was the time religion ruled the world, to be precised, the church. It was in those days when men were beheading in the name of God (which of course is still happening today in the name jihad). When these religious people hear the word CRUSADE, they think it means some church banner's praise and worship, sermon preaching stuffs. Crusading was part of the dark ages when the gospel was spread through blood and sweat. And those who bled by the sword were the men who refused to convert. How can religion be ever forgiven? The church's foundation is built upon genocide, torture, slave trade.

The church, more than any organized institution in the history of mankind, has silenced and spilled the blood of many great scientists, philosophers, and men in the name

God, blasphemy and heresy. Many materials which were educational, has been destroyed in the name of heresy. Men like Galileo learned from this at their own peril. Galileo Galilei who only asserted that the earth is not flat and revolves around the sun was dealt with severely. As matter of fact this is what Cardinal Bellarmine, 1615, during the trial of Galileo said:

"To assert the earth revolves around the sun is erroneous as to claim that Jesus was not born of a virgin." Now we can understand why Galileo who must have been frustrated with such tom-foolery and said: **"Of all the hatred, none is greater than that of ignorance against knowledge."**

Now that we know Galileo was right, shouldn't the church also admit also that Jesus (if he ever existed) was not born of a virgin? It is in the same spirit of arrogance of ignorance that led Sheik Abdel-Aziz ibn Baaz, (Saudi Arabia's supreme religious authority, 1993-1999) to declare **"The earth is flat, and anyone who disputes this claim is an atheist who deserves to be punished."**

The barbarism and crass arrogance of ignorance of the religious has made the time of their glory to be termed a dark age. In 2007, Christopher Hitchens was at a radio studio in Dublin debating with Roman Catholic Church spokesman. How fortunate of him to do that, for it were in the dark ages, Hitchens and this Son of David right here would be burned at stake or beheaded to the glory of the Jewish Janitor (well, it still happens in Iraq by the ISIS, it happens in Saudi Arabia where atheism is a crime, Iran and other places). All assertions and claims of the religious have been disclaimed and proven false through science today, that is why religion never liked science one bit but they'll still want to use scientific inventions to spread their fallacies like going on TV and radio, using the microphone and digital devices to broadcast that Science is an enemy of God and that only Jesus can save but in the end they'll end up going to the hospital when they are sick. When they get well, they come again and say it's Jesus that healed them.

Religion is anti-education. The reason why the so called missionaries built schools was to institutionalized and inculcate their doctrines into the minds of children. Religion only survives through the indoctrination of children who'll be raised into zombies in their adulthood. These schools don't uphold evolution, they uphold creationism, the same goes to the Islamic schools, and they are all built to promote their doctrines using pseudo-science and made-up garbage to support their own personal claims. Education is no education if an individual is taught to think only in a certain type of way. The countries with the highest rates of illiteracy and lowest IQs are the religious nations; let me now ask, of what impact is their so called pseudo-education?

It is absolutely false and wishful to think that any religion contributed to science, art, engineering, math or any other higher subjects of study. The facts that it is flesh, blood and sweats of men and women who contributed solely on the basis of their skills, knowledge, intelligence and research makes it an attribute of the intellect and hard work. Nobody went to the moon through quoting verses in the Quran, neither was the telephone invented through reading the bible. We do not build bridges and palatial structures through the recitation of prayers. As a matter of fact religion and science is like water and oil; they are incompatible. Religion hates sciences passively and often displays some form of insecurity and nausea at scientific inventions and theories that do not augur well with their doctrines. Another synonym for religion should be "anti-science", even till date their nausea for scientific gains and knowledge never seizes, for example rejecting evolution, limiting stem-cell research and multiple other inventions and research on the basis of "playing God" or acting against God. In many instances religion uses the work of science to cause so much evil and spread its virus, like using guns and bombs for terrorism, using the social media and gadgets to spread falsehood, ignorance and fear in their minds of people.

"The world suffers a lot not because of the violence of evil people, but because of the silence of good people"- Napoleon Bonaparte.

FINAL NOTE

The literature icon Oscar Wilde cautioned: "If you want to tell people the truth, make them laugh, otherwise they'll kill you." Sadly, in religion, there is no comedy and humor in telling the religious the truth. Whether you joke about it or not, they won't find it funny and of course, if they can, they will kill you. And for this very reason, this makes religion a monstrous enterprise that is out to secure its fields at whatever cost and whatever means necessary. This alone is enough reason to argue that the world will be a much saner and safer place without religion.

Where all is plain, there is nothing to be argued.

Anytime I come across an enthusiastic preacher or religious apologist who attempts to preach his sermon to me, when I tell them I don't believe in their tales, the utter shock and offense they display when I express my opinion to them is what I am yet to comprehend. What I never understand is why one's disbelief in a God is so offensive to anyone. I don't believe in Santa Claus but I don't run over to my neighbors and tell them to take it down. It's not the belief in God that is necessarily offensive. What is offensive are the things that the belief in a God makes people to do and say: Condemning non-believers, passing legislation to align with their religious beliefs, teaching creationism and religious myth in schools, carrying out acts of terrorism, telling children that they will burn in hell, human rights abuse (including women and children) and condemning the vast majority of the human race to eternal torture in the name of the propagated God are but a few of the things that many of the rational and irreligious people find offensive.

Try to use Santa's naughty/nice list as a method of forming

public policy and I bet rational people will have a problem with it.

> **"Those who are able to see beyond the shadows and lies of their culture will never be understood, let alone be believed by the masses"- Plato**

It is easy to imagine that your religious sensibilities and feelings may have been offended by the thoughts of my ink. If you get mad about a statement of fact, then your emotional reaction isn't my fault. If facts do not align with your beliefs, correct them.

If you are more offended by the sight of a burning Koran or Bible, than the sight of a beheaded or burning human being say a witch or prostitute (because I understand they are like the most terrible nouns in religion), a wild animal in the bush is a better entity than you.

If you are more offended by the news of a burning church and mosque than the news of starving children and hungry people.....

If you think that someone like me is a very terrible human being and I deserve to die because I do not believe there is an imaginary old man in the sky, because I think that hospitals and schools should be developed than extortion and fraudulent buildings called religious centres......

If you think it is a terrible notion as I've conceived that people should be educated with real knowledge and science and religious books should be kept away from schools and it is better to give people a means of livelihood than fantasy messages.......

If you think that a man who slaps a woman for saying she is a "witch for Christ", is a much better human being than myself and anyone who concocts a spurious title of "Man of God" is immune from laws, rules, scrutiny and someone like me who spots their trash will be punished by your imaginary sky genie as "justice" and I'll probably be burned eternally in some hell fire for this, then you are part of the most terrible problems on earth.

Sorry to announce this to you if you fall into this category, you are anything but humane, as such, cannot be called a human being and you have no morality in you!

I don't care about your beliefs. Beliefs are not humans. Beliefs do not have life without you, the believer. Your beliefs need a human in order to survive and not the human in need of a belief in order to survive. For without you, your belief is nothing, so why should I value that which is not, without you above you, who is, even without it?

I do not care whatever anyone believes in, as long as his belief is not making him constitute a problem to me and my environment. Nobody would have complained if someone was worshipping his thing in his room. If I worship my rabbit at home, nobody will be disturbed about it, but they'll be problems if I leave my home and start causing discomfort for others and cursing them that they must worship my rabbit or I'll start making laws in my country from my "RABBITISM". They would have been no problem about religion or religious people if the religious people were not causing problems for both themselves and others.

Religion is a dangerous tripe such that, talking about it and criticizing it can get you killed. And that makes it certainly evil, as the German thinker, Friedrich Nietzsche noted: **"Sometimes people don't want to hear the truth because they don't want their illusions destroyed."** When people start murdering each other over a difference in mathematics or science, the religious apologists will have room to claim they are peaceful. When you hear a group of biologists declare war on Physicists, and astro-physicists condemn aeronautic engineers to eternal torture, the religious can come out and play with ridicule at science. Until then religion should be regarded as an embarrassment to the collective senses of mankind. When you subscribe to religion, you subscribe to a fallacious hallucinogenic stimulant. And that's all you need to start committing all kinds of fantastic fatalism. Religion must be eradicated or brought to the barest minimum if mankind wants to live at peace with one another. Religion is the best reason people will hate each other over nothing. I have lost many friends because I no longer subscribe to any religion. I have never met anyone who said he stopped becoming friends with another because he switched from his former NBA team say Chicago bulls to LA Lakers. I have never heard that a group of people began fighting because one switch from studying biology to studying physics.

I will never accept any religion or philosophical ideology that demoralizes my cultural identity and castrates my rationality. If there is a God, it will be most likely that he will be more than irritated by people who claim he exists and have the so called knowledge of him and yet can't proof beyond reasonable doubt that he truly exists. If he exists, I'm sure he has a lot of respect for those who ridicule those who claim to know him, and he is more likely to be disgusted by the folks who do not use the brain he gave them to reason this mess out. And again, if he exists, he'll be more than entertained and glorified by the wits, guts and most importantly, the refusal of the free-thinker and the irreligious to be subjected to buffoonery. Finally, if there was some after-life and reward, he'll be more than willing to share the same abode with people who lived up to the standard of the homosapien by being sapient in all matters, especially those that concern his name. However, if by chance he exists and he is exactly the way the holy books authored by men describe him and ascribes his intelligence to be, then he is absolutely a junk-headed disappointment of a being. The good thing is that he is fictious.

With the bombings all around the world, the persecutions, discrimination, and all manner of chaos in the name of God and religion, I have just this one prayer: "Oh God, protect me from your followers."

www.ingramcontent.com/pod-product-compliance
Lightning Source LLC
Chambersburg PA
CBHW062207080426
42734CB00010B/1823